D1095801

MUST YOU CONFORM?

Books by Robert Lindner

REBEL WITHOUT A CAUSE
STONE WALLS AND MEN
PRESCRIPTION FOR REBELLION
THE FIFTY-MINUTE HOUR: *A Collection of True Psychoanalytic Tales*
MUST YOU CONFORM?

• • • •

HANDBOOK OF CORRECTIONAL PSYCHOLOGY
(ed. with R. V. Seliger)
CONTEMPORARY CRIMINAL HYGIENE
(ed. with R. V. Seliger and E. J. Lukas)
EXPLORATIONS IN PSYCHOANALYSIS (ed.)

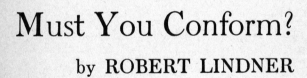

Must You Conform?

by ROBERT LINDNER

RINEHART & COMPANY, INC.
NEW YORK
TORONTO

Published simultaneously in Canada by
Clarke, Irwin & Company, Ltd., Toronto

© 1956 by Robert Lindner
Printed in the United States of America
Library of Congress Catalog Card Number: 55-10528

TO PHILIP LAWRENCE HARRIMAN,

TEACHER AND FRIEND

Foreword

THE COLLECTION OF ESSAYS YOU ARE ABOUT TO READ HAS HAD A CURIOUS HISTORY. WHEN FOUR OF THEM —"The Mutiny of the Young," "The Instinct of Rebellion," "Must You Conform?" and "Education for Maturity"—were presented in Los Angeles as The Hacker Foundation Lectures for 1954 during November of that year, they immediately aroused a storm of controversy. Among the approximately two thousand people who attended that series of lectures, opinion was divided sharply. Some were outraged by the theme of these four pieces, alienated by the thesis around which they were composed, and provoked to bitter comment by the ideas they contain. Others, however, although not necessarily in agreement with everything I said, were pleased to hear some of their own thoughts formulated and presented from a public platform. I left Los Angeles happy in the conviction —supported by many letters, telephone calls and newspaper comments—that I had at least excited a small but unusually intelligent group to think further about vital issues. Before departing, however, I promised my friend, Dr. Frederick J. Hacker, the distinguished psychiatrist who heads The Hacker Foundation and Clinic, that I would someday publish the lectures he had so graciously sponsored.

Some two weeks after I returned to Baltimore, *Time Magazine* published an excellent summation of "The Mutiny of the Young" in its section on Medicine. I was hardly prepared for what followed. Within three days, both the postman and I had cause to regret *Time's* action; over five hundred letters were received, and editors from all over the United States wrote or phoned, requesting the original essay on which *Time* had reported. Approximately forty newspapers devoted editorial space to the points raised in the article, and in at least five instances known to me prolonged debate was carried on in the columns of leading metropolitan dailies like the *Washington Post and Times Herald.* For months, thereafter, I was kept busy revising and repeating these four lectures to various audiences, seminars, study groups and organizations. Accordingly, "The Mutiny of the Young" has been presented four times as of this date (including one notable occasion in Washington, D.C., when an eminent but irate jurist, severely shaken by what he heard, so far forgot his dignity as to shout at me: "Sir, I have committed many men to our public institutions for saying less dangerous things than you did tonight!"). "The Instinct of Rebellion" has been given three times; once as the Annual Phi Beta Kappa Address at

Bucknell University, and twice to psychological col-
loquia. "Must You Conform?" has also been heard
three times; at the Sixth Annual Conference of Parents
and Teachers of the Oak Lane Country Day School of
Temple University, at a public meeting sponsored by
The Nassau County Psychological Association, and at
Princeton University. And "Education for Maturity"
has been offered on a number of instances, the most
memorable being as the Commencement Address to
the graduates of The Park School in Baltimore.

"Homosexuality and the Contemporary Scene" is
derived from a paper, otherwise entitled, originally
prepared for delivery to the Southern California
Chapter of Correctional Service Associates and presented as part of their Guest Lecturer Series in Los
Angeles on November 5, 1954. Although often requested to repeat the article or print it, I have delayed
its publication until now because it fits so well the
theme of this book and makes a necessary transition
between its parts. Moreover, I felt an additional period
to contemplate and substantiate my thinking in this
complex area was imperative.

The remaining essay, "Political Creed and Character," has been printed before in a slightly different
form. Originally two long chapters from a projected
work on "Psychopolitics," it was published in the Winter, 1953 issue of *Psychoanalysis: The Journal of Psychoanalytic Psychology*. Previous to its appearance
there, however, a foreshortened version was recorded
for *Sound Seminars*. Following its publication in *Psy-*

choanalysis, moreover, yet another rendering was circulated privately and on request, among officials at
Radio Free Europe, editors of certain opinion-making
magazines, and experts in foreign affairs. Shortly after
reprints of the article were made available, urgent re-
quests for permission to print in translation were received from the editors of three foreign psychoanalyt-
ical journals. Although such permission was granted
gladly, in all three countries the article met with the
same fate. Due to strenuous objections raised by certain political elements in the societies sponsoring the
journals involved, in each case the article had to be
withdrawn; in one of these instances, parenthetically,
the entire issue of the particular journal was torn down
and remade at considerable expense to the faction that
found it objectionable. I am, therefore, grateful to the
editors of *Psychoanalysis* for granting me permission
to republish "Political Creed and Character" here
(with a few changes) and thankful to be a citizen of a
country where it is still possible for a man to write as
he pleases.

The essays that follow are thematically bound by
their common attempt to formulate and answer the
problem of conformity. In a series of ever-widening
progressions, from the personal and intimate to the
socio-political and universal, I have tried to explore
the dimensions of the most vital issue of our era and,
subsequently, to offer those replies and solutions that
suggest themselves to the psychologically oriented ob-

server. To some extent, I regard this volume as a continuation of my PRESCRIPTION FOR REBELLION, wherein
I was concerned chiefly with exposing the myth of adjustment. There, however, I was preoccupied with the
effects of that myth and its conformist implications
upon the science and arts of psychology. Herein, it is
the entire human condition that commands attention.

"Must you conform?" is the question that haunts
all men living in this time of crisis and decision. Upon
the collective answer we make to this query rests the
fate of our social order and the destiny of our children.
It is my fervent hope that the thoughts on these pages
will assist toward making a correct reply.

Robert Lindner

Baltimore
October, 1955

Contents

The Mutiny of the Young

I.

IT IS A COMMONPLACE OF FOLK-WISDOM THAT
THE STATE OF YOUTH IS ALWAYS AND EVERYWHERE ONE
of rebellion. This is something that every adult ex-
pects and accepts. Recalling his own adolescence,
each parent resigns himself to a period of distressful
concern, ordinarily of predictable length, when his
child will pass through a state of active insurrection,
when his offspring will flaunt convention, dispute authority, and vigorously, if at times rather recklessly,
oppose the institutions that traditionally regulate society.

This rebellion of youth is acknowledged all over
the earth. It is tolerated by all cultures. The most
rigid of primitive societies acquiesce in it, and there
even exist, among certain exotic communities, social
mechanisms that not only provide for but encourage
and assist adolescent revolt in its expression. In some
places, under the guise of initiatory rites of passage
from childhood to manhood, an astonishing degree of
permissiveness in behavior is granted youth. This lati-

3

tude constitutes at once an admission of the facts of adolescence and a technique of management. We of Western civilization, however, cannot permit ourselves the moral laxity implicit in numerous Oriental and Pacific proverbs that counsel relaxation in the face of the inevitable: for us it remains unthinkable to formalize—and by formalizing to accept as a social reality—anything so potentially disruptive, so flagrantly opposed to the sense of sin with which our philosophers tell us we are burdened. Nevertheless, in an informal (one might almost say underground) way, we do admit, and through an increasingly large range of our behavior sanction, a kind of "free" period for youth, a Roman holiday, a time when the excesses, follies and renegadism of the young are regarded benignly.

Throughout all levels of our Western society there may be observed a wry and amused sufferance of the rebellious adolescent, and an almost pitifully conscientious attempt to "understand"—and so forgive—his disquieting behavior. Not only parents, but also the delegates of social agencies, exhibit wide permissiveness in the affair. Officialdom agrees with the distilled experience of the race: that there is and should be a time when youth, responding to some wild trumpet call of the blood, *must* flex its muscles, *must* try to throw off the yoke. And so the face of officialdom, too, assumes a regretful, self-conscious smile, and for a brief while authority withholds its heavy hand.

Nor do science and art neglect the matter. The former, forever re-discovering with wide-eyed naïveté what everyman already knows by instinct, seeks to explain—and so to rationalize—the period of protest. It speaks of glandular processes that underwrite waywardness, of hormonal hurricanes and physiologic phenomena, and, latterly, of common psychic drives that express themselves according to a predictable timetable. As for art, the revolt of the young has always been a favorite theme. From the most ancient scratchings on clay through the Testaments, from the fragmentary runes of nameless bards through the epic poetry of the Greeks, from the earliest romances through the modern novel, play and motion picture runs a persistent if endlessly varied motif: that the sons and daughters of men must and will, at some point previous to the date of full adulthood and maturity, rebel.

Until quite recently the rebellion of youth in the West could be viewed with the detachment usually accorded anything so common and natural. It was possible to accept it, to incorporate it into our knowledge of the world and the behavior of its inhabitants. As adults, we have even come to view it, despite its attendant personal and social distresses, with nostalgia. Unhappily, however, such an attitude of benevolent forbearance and, in some instances, secret complicity, is no longer appropriate . . . *For the brute fact of today is that our youth is no longer in rebellion, but in a condition of downright active and hostile mutiny.*

Semanticists may—and undoubtedly will—object to the distinction to be drawn here between rebellion and mutiny. But neither they nor anyone can dispute that within the memory of every living adult a profound and terrifying change has overtaken the character of that time of life we call adolescence. The matter requires no documentation: a mere glance at the daily news reports from all over the world testifies to its validity. Therein may be read the details of a transformation the consequences of which can be of the greatest significance for the future.

That we may understand what has occurred with our youth, and on the basis of such understanding formulate plans to cope with the situation, it is first necessary to describe, as clearly as we can, the nature of the change I have characterized as a shift from rebellion to mutiny. As a result of rather wide and intensive experience in the area, an experience that includes almost daily contact with young people in schools, clinics, courtrooms, and prisons, I have been impressed by two radical innovations in the psychology of present-day adolescents. I am sure there are other differences between the currently mutinous and formerly rebellious young; but the two that have struck me as outstanding appear not only to reduce the mass of evidence to manageable proportions, but also to provide an explanation for the sorry spectacle we are witnessing.

I have noticed, first of all, that what marks the youth of this day as different from his predecessor is a tendency to *act out*, to display, his inner turmoil. This trend, I think it can be agreed, is in direct contrast to the *suffering out* of the same internal agitation by adolescents of yesteryear. What this means is that there has come about in our young people, for reasons I intend to explore later, a weakening or decay of psychic inhibitors, of mechanisms of control and restraint, so that the felt turbulence of that period of life is immediately translated into overt behavior, and the impulses which were formerly content to remain at the level of pure feeling now receive motor expression.

By way of illustration, two newspaper stories from opposite ends of the earth offer themselves. The first comes from Brooklyn, New York, where four youths were apprehended in the summer of 1954 for committing a series of violent acts that would tax the credulity of all of us had we not already become satiated with similar tales. According to the press these adolescent boys were responsible for a devil's rosary of crimes ranging from rape to murder, and all stamped with an unbelievable degree of sadism. Newspaper and magazine writers described the youngsters as rather "average" pre-adults with origins in "good" middle-class families. They also told us that the outrages perpetrated by these youths seemed, to them at least, "inexplicable" and "senseless," since no evidence existed that the horrors were performed for the "usual motives"—by which I assume they mean such comprehensible motivants of crime as hope of gain or disposal of a threatening enemy.

My other press clipping comes from New Zealand by way of England. It describes the almost inconceivably savage, premeditated murder of a mother by her teen-age daughter assisted by a girl friend for whom the child was supposed to have conceived some unspecified erotic attachment. The young murderess, whose father is a physician and who, apparently, never before exhibited an inclination toward violence, revealed that the killing was prompted by the desire of the girls to remain together. It seems that the family of the friend was planning to move to South Africa, an eventuality which threatened to separate the couple forever unless the victim could be persuaded to permit her child to accompany them. Separation had to be prevented somehow, and murder was the outcome. Those who interviewed the girl in custody, by the way, emphasized her "detachment" and "callous indifference." Both she and her associate, it was said, "exulted over their crime" and "showed no reasonable emotional appreciation of their situation."

Now I would like to offer a contrast between the two news stories just reviewed and the experience of every adult reader. Better still, let us recall from the

world's literature those classical descriptions of adolescent psychology and behavior given by writers of
perception and insight whose accounts of this period
—autobiographical or fictional—mirror so accurately
a time we have all shared. There is no need to name
titles or revive characters: what is necessary is to remember that the storms of adolescence detailed by
Shakespeare, Goethe, Tolstoy, Dostoevsky, Twain,
Dickens, Joyce, Mann and all the rest, were *inward*
storms. Like the four unfortunates from Brooklyn and
the two from New Zealand, these authors or their
characters felt what is common to youth to feel. Lust
was in them, also vast and devouring if nameless hungers, as well as cosmic yearnings, strange thirsts, occult sensations, murderous rages, vengeful fantasies
and imaginings that catalogue all of sin and crime.
But—and here is the point—unlike the sorry six, in
them these impulses were contained within the skin's
envelope, denied access to action, hence merely felt
and suffered in the private agony of a tormenting pre-
adulthood.

Largely, this is precisely what you and I knew as
adolescents—a swelling tide of feeling and solitary
inquietude. What outward expression we did give to
our feelings and impulses was mainly symbolical,
thrice and more removed from those direct acts toward which we may have been impelled. But I write
of a time that has passed, and while I certainly would
not generalize that every adolescent of today has ex-

changed action for suffering, it would be delusion to
fail to recognize a mounting trend toward this unfor-
tunate transaction among our youth.

There is another and equally significant difference between the young mutineer of the present and
his rebellious forebearer. I refer to the abandonment
of that solitude which was at once the trade-mark of
adolescence and the source of its deepest despairs as
of its dubious ecstasies.

If there was anything that used to distinguish the
period of youth from other times in the life of the human animal, it was the privacy, the *aloneness*, of those
fretful years. The emotions I have mentioned were
intimate, the mood was secret, and the temper of the
entire era intensely personal. At most, one or two
close companions shared the occasion; but even in
these instances the participation was limited to mutual enterprises during which the first hesitant experi-
ments with adult behavior were made. What wider
associations were formed by youths were temporary
and often desperate solutions offering easement of a
self-imposed exile; but even here, in the secret societies, the sororities and the confraternities based on
special interests, the personal and intimate, the feeling
side, was reserved to the individual himself as something either too precious or too strange or too extravagant to be shared. And frequently this solitude of
adolescence was creative. From it sometimes came
the dreams, the hopes, and the soaring aims that

charged life henceforward with meaning and contributed toward those fulfillments which have given us our poets, artists, scientists, and productive persons in all fields.

But, again, what we observe today is otherwise. Youth has abandoned solitude: it has relinquished privacy. Instead, these are the days of pack-running, of predatory assembly, of organization into great collectivities that bury, if they do not destroy, individuality. And it is into these mindless associations that the young flock like cattle. More than their privacy, the fee they pay for initiation is abandonment of self and immersion in the herd, with its consequent sacrifice of personality.

Once more, it should be remarked that the phenomenon is not local but universal. In England, for example, there are the *Edwardians*, noted especially for their dress and the style of life they practice. The following is quoted from a letter I received recently:

> You ask me to tell you about the Edwardians. Well, perhaps this will do. They are, first of all, the queerest ever in their mode of dress. If you will look in your family album, I am sure you will find a photograph of the period they profess to imitate. It is all there. Believe it or not, that is exactly how they dress.
>
> As a psychiatrist, however, I am much more interested in their manner. They conscientiously affect an attitude of boredom and disdain, from which they are aroused only by an occasion for violence. By every line of their

usual posture, a sort of round-shouldered
lounge on the edge of total collapse, they show
their contempt for the rest of us. It is too early
to tell yet what their code consists of, or what
their values may be. In respect of sex, I am told,
they have a troubadour-like attachment to one
girl but consider all other females fair game and
hunt in packs, winding up in orgies that in my
time were called "gang-shags". The knife is
their favorite weapon, together with the black-
jack and rubber hose. They are said to be
tightly organized and to communicate by a set
of signals involving the eyes, hands, and collo-
quialisms similar to your "jive-talk".

In the Soviet Union there are the *bezprizornye*
or "homeless." Here is what Gustav Herling has to say
about them in his remarkable book, *A World Apart:*

> Juvenile delinquents, like the boys in the
> cell, are the plague of the Soviet prisons, though
> they are almost never found in labor camps.
> Unnaturally excited, always ferreting in other
> men's bunks and inside their own trousers, they
> give themselves up passionately to the only two
> occupations of their lives, theft and self-abuse.
> Almost all of them either have no parents or else
> know nothing of their whereabouts. Through-
> out the vast expanse of the Russian Police State
> they manage to lead with astounding ease the
> typical life of "bezprizornye", jumping freight
> trains, constantly on the move from town to
> town, from settlement to settlement. They make
> a living by stealing and selling goods from gov-

ernment stores, and frequently they steal back
what they have just sold, blackmailing unsus-
pecting purchasers with the threat of laying information against them. They sleep in railway
stations, in municipal parks, in streetcar termi-
nals; often all their belongings can be wrapped
in a small bundle tied with a leather strap. Only
later I discovered that the bezprizornye consti-
tute a most dangerous semi-legal mafia, organized on the pattern of Masonic lodges, and sur-
passed only by the more powerful organizations
of "urkas" or criminal prisoners. If in Russia
anything like a black market exists, it is only
thanks to the efforts of these urchins, always
weaving in and out of crowds, besieging the
"spectorgs" (special shops supplying exclusively
the *élite* of the Soviet bureaucracy), creeping at
dusk toward stores of corn and coal. The Soviet
authorities wink at all this activity; they regard
the bezprizornye as the only true proletariat
free of the original sin of counter-revolution, as
a plastic mass of raw material which can be
molded into any shape they choose.

In the United States, of course, we have had a
long history of juvenile gangs which are the bane of
every large city. Los Angeles, for instance, is supposed to contain many such organizations of which
the estimated total membership is at least five thousand. Composed predominantly of teen-agers, these
groups, each numbering from twenty to about one
hundred, practice every known vice and are presumably guilty of crimes ranging from thievery to mur-

der. The names they sport tell little or nothing about them: such designations as the Rose Hill, Dogtown, White Fence, Honey Dripped, Valley Cutdowns, Little First Street, etc., fail to reveal their true pre-occupations, which seem to be the use and peddling of narcotics, thievery, armed robbery, criminal attacks on women, and murder by knife, gun, or brutal beat-ing. According to reliable accounts, members of such gangs and others elsewhere are strictly disciplined, and violations of the gang code may—and often do—result in death.

More recently in this country, however, we have been presented with a new phenomenon similar in form to the *Edwardians* of England, the *bezprizornye* of the Soviet Union, and the *Steppenwolfen* of Ger-many. The *Pachucos,* with their identifying tattoo, their code of violence and their uniform dress, seem to be spreading everywhere and welding the hitherto warring gangs into a solid front associated for com-mon criminal purposes. While this movement is still in its infancy—at least as far as the forces of legality are able to discover—it or something like it bids fair to become the mold from which the mutinous pattern of the young is to be cast in future.

The innovation distinguishing the modern ado-lescent, which I have described as the abandonment of privacy, has far-reaching implications. One of them is certainly the fact that it can yield no social gain. Nothing creative can possibly come from it, for it is in solitude that the works of hand, heart and mind are always conceived, and in solitude that individuality must be affirmed. In addition, we hardly need to be reminded that in the crowd, herd, or gang, it is a mass-mind that operates—which is to say, a mind without subtlety, a mind without compassion, a mind, finally, uncivilized. This type of mind is the perfect instrument for the direction of a kind of behavior which, circumventing the deeper feelings, expresses abruptly and brutally, upon the body of society, the troubled souls of today's children.

II.

During the past decades, while the pattern of what I have called the mutiny of the young was taking final shape, an anxious and concerned public has been seeking guidance. The social physicians they have consulted have, unfortunately, failed them. Instead of diagnosing the trouble correctly and prescribing appropriate remedies, our experts have thus far produced only absurd theories and warmed-over nostrums which do little more than compound confusion. Besieged by such social and psychiatric palliatives as "throw away the comic books," "close down the television stations," "return to breast-feeding," and "get tough with them,"—and too often in the same moment advised exactly to the contrary—

harassed parents, distraught teachers and bewildered public servants understandably surrender to apathy.

The problem of youth in mutiny is acute and profound. Bearing as it does on the character of the future, it demands immediate attention. But, as will be seen, it takes courage to face up to the challenge it presents, courage even to view the situation in its true perspective, and boldness to act as the condition demands.

Really to understand what is happening to youth all over the earth requires, first of all, a sense of history and a world view that sets current happenings in the context of the past. It requires, also, the exercise of sufficient prophetic ability to comprehend correctly and foresee the march of events toward a future the outlines of which are already visible. It requires, finally, a psychological sapience that clarifies the motives of men and discerns at least the nature of the unconscious forces by which they are driven.

In the first part of this discussion, you will recall, it was found possible to reduce many if not all of the characteristics displayed by so many of our modern adolescents to two rather comprehensive yet basic propositions: (1) that they are prone to act out, in the theatre of society, those impulses which arise from internal distress; and (2) that they tend to drift into, or merge with, herd-like collectivities in which individuality is lost and the direction of activities is taken over by a group mind. I now propose to treat both of these incontestable phenomena clinically, and to show that they are symptoms of a psychiatric condition, world-wide in scope, and related directly to the social and political temper of our times.

I am sure that I have been anticipated in the diagnosis of the modern adolescent by the psychological sophisticates among my readers. There is only one mental aberration in which the two symptoms I have described co-exist. I refer, of course, to the psychiatric classification of *psychopathic personality,* a form of disorder that renders its victims essentially antisocial, conscienceless, inclined to violence in behavior, and liable to loss of identity in the group, gang, mob, or herd.

The psychopath is, as I have often pointed out, a rebel without a cause, hence an individual who is in a chronic state of mutiny. He strives solely for the satisfaction of his moment-to-moment desires, and since these are the satisfactions of the very earliest period of life, they are impossible to attain. His urges, therefore, are primitive to the utmost degree, and the methods by which he seeks to realize them, patterned on the methods available to him in infancy, are also primitive. Raw need is all that drives him; raw need that originated in the cradle, prior to the formation of conscience, before the birth of all except the monomaniacal feelings, antecedent to the knowledge of the presence of others in the world, and previous to the establishment of such social inhibitors as guilt, shame, and love that is not of the self.

Outstanding in the psychopath, in this mutineer in our midst, are the very characteristics which mark, to one degree or another, more and more of our youth. For the psychopath, more than anyone, in obedience to primal inner stresses, acts—violently, swiftly, without forethought and in a fashion every observer would describe (as the deeds of the sorry six were described above) as senseless. He experiences emotion, of course, but he has no tolerance for it, nor does he know it in its subtler forms. At once, and without mediation of reason or the civilized concerns common to all but the most primitive of men, he translates the stress of emotion to behavior. And his tendency to seek his like in the wolf-pack, as we find our adolescents doing increasingly these days, is too obvious to require other than passing comment, except to note how in the pack his unique status as an individual, as a person, disappears.

I could elaborate further on the resemblance between the modern adolescent and the psychopath, but there is little need to labor the point. Compare, if you will, the classical description of psychopathy from any standard psychiatric textbook with the graphic sketches in news reports of a growing number of youths who behave in ways that bring them to public attention; better still, compare the textbook portrait with what you observe about your own or your neighbor's child . . . and you will be appalled by the result. Almost every symptom that delineates the psychopath clinically is to be found increasingly

in the contemporary adolescent; but of the greatest prominence and most dire significance are those two which are *never* absent from the clinical specimen and, latterly, *hardly* ever absent from more and more of our young. These, I believe, clinch the diagnosis. They enable us to state, without equivocation, that the youth of the world today is touched with madness, literally sick with an aberrant condition of mind formerly confined to a few distressed souls but now epidemic over the earth.

It is proper to inquire, here, how they got that way. To do this, however, we must take our eyes from the microscope through which we have been examining our children, and lift them to survey the world.

What immediately impresses itself upon the enlarged screen of our observation is that it is not youth alone that has succumbed to the form of insanity we clinicians label psychopathy, but nations, populations —indeed, the whole of mankind. For at least thirty years, and perhaps more, our civilization has been demonstrating behavior that, were the same to be discovered in the solitary human being, would cause the forces concerned with public order and safety speedily to remove him to an asylum for the mentally deranged. The world, in short, has run amuck. As a species, we are exhibiting exactly what the most profoundly disturbed psychopathic personality shows. Like him, we are without conscience and given to violence. Like him, we are predatory and selfish. Like

him, we are without feelings and must have what we want when we want it. Like him, we have given up our identity as individuals and do not respect the rights and privileges of others . . . But why continue? The whole tale is contained in a few geographic place names—Madrid, Munich, Buchenwald, Warsaw, Hiroshima, Kargopol, Los Alamos, Seoul, Hanoi . . .

But if this is madness, what is its source? What has made Western man the ravening psychotic he has become?

If, as I believe, we are in the midst of an epidemic of psychopathy, if it is this disorder which has seized the race and is being communicated to our children, then a clue to the answer to these questions may be found in the psychodynamics of the disease.

Let us begin by noting that psychopathy is, first of all, a condition that is latent in all of us. Because we were all infants, and the infant is the prototype of the psychopath, none of us is immune from the disorder and all of us, at one time or another, behave psychopathically. Obviously, the infant cannot be called a psychopath, since his behavior is natural to his stage of life. However, when, for any reason, a person regresses in his behavior to infancy, when he expresses infantile aims and seeks their realization by infantile techniques, he earns the diagnosis. To elaborate, let us consider the following: barring organic and psychic inferiority, injury or disease, it is a reasonable presumption that as time goes on the individual will

manifest certain specific changes to indicate the passing of infancy. He will acquire control over his urges, the more selfish drives will become channelized, defenses will be erected against his transitory impulses, and curbs will be placed upon his immediate desires. But when he fails to accomplish these desirable changes, if he never shows these attributes in his behavior, or if he reverts to behavior that clearly indicates these attributes are no longer operative—then the label of psychopathy can be applied.

Now, it has been well established that there are two ways of producing a psychopath. The first is by failure or fault in the developmental course of the individual life. For various reasons which need not concern us here, the normal progress of the child from stage to stage in his emotional development is prevented, and he carries over into chronological adulthood all the reactions proper to the infant. He becomes, in brief, an infant in the body of an adult.

The second way in which the psychopath is produced is more relevant to our discussion. By this method, the state of psychopathy is brought about by damage to the ego, which is the keystone in the arch of personality. Anything which debilitates that ego, anything which renders the self weak or destroys its integrity, exposes the latent infantilism never far below the surface in any case, producing regression to an earlier pattern of behavior marked by the disappearance of the attributes of maturation.

The world of the decades that comprise the first half of this Twentieth Century has provided stimuli for ego-weakening in abundance. In the huge power presses that mask as political parties, through the vast processes that characterize what may be the final convulsions of a society, the integrity of each individual has been ground to dust. Millions of men, as catastrophes and cataclysms signalized by wars and economic upheavals fell upon them, have been displaced. Their identities as persons have been lost or stolen. And with the displacement, the dispossession and the loss of identity, has come insecurity. Finally, as the maggot appears in the rotting flesh, insecurity has bred the soul-destroying plague we know as mass psychopathy. To this downward progression mutely testify cattle car and crematorium, slave-labor stockade and the bitter road of exile.

As we, in our timidity of thought and psychological naïveté, have confused results with causes in desperate attempts to account for the distress of youth—indicting comic books, television, Hollywood films, etc.—so have we erred in mistaking results for causes in that larger area of universal distress: the total human scene. Misled by the easy equations of certain sociologists, the ambiguous correlations of some historians, and the pre-digested formulations of the Marxists, we have missed the signs that point to a deeper source for our adversity. We have failed to grasp the evidence that indicates so clearly that the sands of our civilization's time are running out; that the plague of psychopathic behavior that sickens us is the chief symptom of our society's expiring agony; that what is happening now has happened before and will probably happen again and again and yet again —until mankind awakens to knowledge of himself.

I will not weary you with a recital here of the psychological theory of history that leads to the conclusions I have drawn. In my book, *Prescription for Rebellion* (Rinehart, 1952), a more detailed but still highly inadequate presentation of it can be found. Let it suffice, for this essay, to state my conviction that as a consequence of complex historical and psychological forces our civilization appears to have entered its terminal phase. Eminently if not chiefly characteristic of this phase is the increasing presence among us of Mass Men and the rapid conversion of all the human units of our society to Mass Manhood.

The Mass Man, of course, is the psychopath *in excelsis*. A mechanized, robotized caricature of humanity, it is he who finally tears down around his own head the house of his culture. A slave in mind and body, whose life signifies no more than an instrument of his masters' power, a lost creature without separate identity in the herding collectivity, a mindless integer of the pack who wakens from his torpor only when prodded by the whip from outside or the stab of brute appetite from within, it is he who finally inherits the earth and runs it to ruin.

III.

In the perspective I have just outlined the mutiny of the young takes on an entirely different significance. No longer can we regard it as the product of "bad" influences, a transient perversity of youth that time will cure, or a few applications of social-service soporifics and mental-hygiene maxims fix. In this perspective, the eighteen-year-old from Massachusetts who, in July of 1954, killed his mother's dressmaker, age fifty-two, by strangling her manually, beating her repeatedly on the head with a rolling pin, and stabbing her in the chest with a six-and-one-half-inch bread knife; and the twelve-year-old with a brace of pistols and fifty rounds of ammunition who fought it out against fifteen policemen in Colorado in October, finally surrendering with the taunt, "I hate cops"—assume an import that reaches far beyond them. Now they and their violent deeds appear as possible specimens of the shape of things to come, as likely models of an emergent type of humanity and harbingers of the time of troubles that perhaps awaits the species. To continue to regard them through the inverted telescope that reduces this significance, to employ the usual feeble weapons and techniques in a matter that so clearly involves human destiny, is to stumble blindly toward a meeting with disaster. "Better" schools will not help, nor will more stringent laws, harsher punishments, the Boy Scouts, Police Athletic Leagues, Visiting Teacher programs, social work in distressed areas, Big Brother movements, nor, indeed, any of the pitiful remedies customarily prescribed for ordinary ailments of the social body.

I wish with all my heart that I did not have to write these pessimistic lines. As a parent, I would like to believe that the three girls in Baltimore who were exposed last year as operators of a vice-center and heroin "drop" for teen-agers were extreme but isolated instances, no more than casualties, perhaps, of broken homes, parental neglect, poverty, or any of the thousand simple social equations available to us. As a clinician, I wish I could devise some magical technique, or at least advise a program of action based on the standard faiths of my craft—advocate, possibly, a return to religion, a restoration of the power of positive thinking, a universal lobotomy, or an easy method to make the mind mature. But I cannot, as parent or clinician, believe in the isolation of the Baltimore adolescents in the face of overwhelming evidence to the contrary, nor can I counsel against the dictates of my knowledge. For the fact of the matter is that the mutiny of the young is not an ordinary social ailment, but a virulent epidemic affecting the race of man. And the further fact of the matter is that every medicine available to our social physicians and so far prescribed by them has sped, rather than

checked, the progress of the disease from which we
are dying.

I suggest that we are attempting to solve the
plight of youth by the very methods that have conspired to loose a reign of death and terror upon the
world. I suggest that we are every day creating anew
and compounding the conditions that generate the
psychopathic virus and cause it to flourish. I suggest
that everything we have done and are doing to combat the rising epidemic I have described only spreads
the infection.

Mass Man, the universal psychopath, is born
when the individual ego is weakened to the point at
which it loses separate identity and is forced, for security, to merge with the mass. This becomes possible, however, only when what I believe to be a
fundamental instinct of the human animal is outraged
or betrayed. There is that within us that cannot be
denied without destroying the essence of humanity.
It is a drive to master, to overcome, to express positive protest against whatever stands in the way of
the far-off and unknown goals of evolution. When
this in-built urge is impeded or suppressed, the qualities that make up the humanity of man disappear,
and in the place of a man stands a goose-stepping
automaton driven by animal lusts.

The betrayal of the instinct that has enabled man
to rise up from the primeval swamp is accomplished
by the spread of a myth that enervates the species;
a myth that urges us ever closer to the edge of an
abyss in which lie the wrecks of former civilizations

that have succumbed to it. I refer to the myth of
conformity, the big lie of *adjustment*.

In the time of their demise, it has been characteristic of all peoples that they have surrendered to pressures put upon them by their power-mad leaders, by
their insane religions, and by their misguided philosophies to conform. Protest becomes outlawed,
submission the chief of the virtues, and the expression
of individuality by word or act a cardinal sin. But
because it is not in the nature of man to submit, because it violates his instinct to forego protest, an
intolerable tension arises within him. Forced from
without to conform, and from within to rebel, he
makes a compromise: he rebels within the confines of
conformity, he discharges his protest within the limits set by the social order he has by now permitted
to be erected around him. Just so does he become
transformed into storm-trooper, blackshirt, N.K.V.D.
inquisitor, guard on the long march from Corregidor,
or burner of the fiery cross. And just so is the world he
makes transformed into a giant Lubianka and an immense Dachau.

It becomes evident, now, how we err in our efforts to stem the tide of psychopathy among the
young, and how futile are the methods we employ.
For almost every scheme, every plan, every proposal,
every invention we have so far devised *against* their
mutiny serves, instead, to encourage it. There exists
—and I state this categorically—there exists *nothing*
which does not require the young to conform, to adjust, to submit, to become regimented. Examine re-

ligion, education, psychology, social work, philosophy, recreation, pediatrics . . . each is infused with
the rot-producing idea that the salvation of individual
and of society depends upon conformity and adjustment. And this is the very soil in which psychopathy
and Mass Manhood take root and grow. Until we
reach a clear understanding of these destructive processes and learn at last not to place the foundations of
our culture on the quicksand of myth, we can expect
only increasing distress and, eventually, social death
from the miasma that rises from that soil, from the
germ that our devotion to error spreads.

Our adolescents reflect the slow but ominous advance of a psychic contagion. They are but one step
forward from us along the road to Mass Manhood.
Into them we have bred our fears and insecurities,
upon them we have foisted our mistakes and miscon-
ceptions. In our stead they are expressing the unre-
lieved rage, the constricting tension and the terrible
frustration of the world they were born into. Their
revolt, as much as the world they face, is not of their
making. They are helpless and hopeless, imprisoned
by the blunders and delusions of their predecessors;
and like all prisoners, they are mutineers in their
hearts. Pathetically, and against the rising wind, they
cry out with the late George Orwell, "But at any rate
this was the great, abiding lesson of my boyhood: that
I was in a world where it was *not possible* for me to
be good."

Homosexuality and the Contemporary Scene

I.

It is widely held that modern society is undergoing a sexual revolution. Many people believe that since the close of World War I, at least, sex attitudes and behavior reveal a radical and progressive change. Among the examples they usually employ to document this belief, they offer the homosexual and what they describe as a novel and more healthy social disposition toward him. No longer a pariah, a despised and cast-off sub-man whose sexual proclivities are to be regarded with disgust and whose person is to be avoided, he is, so these enthusiasts tell us, "accepted, tolerated, and understood."

I, for one, do not believe that we are in the midst of, or have even begun to have, a sexual revolution. The evidence that confronts me daily is all to the contrary. Despite the open sale of contraceptives, the spate of books and pamphlets offering sexual information, the prevalence of four-letter words in novels,

plays and verbal intercourse, the widespread use of
sex-educational films in classrooms, and the Bikini
bathing suit, I and most of my colleagues in psychoanalysis still find the situation as regards sex repressive. Fundamental attitudes seem not to have altered
significantly, certainly not since the middle of the
Nineteenth Century. The same fears persist and the
same fictions prevail. For us, and for all others who
deal intimately with people, the popularization of sex
and the appearance of liberalism in attitude and behavior represent little more than flourishing defenses
—reaction-formations, rationalizations, denials, etc.—
against deeply embedded conflicts between the erotic
instincts and the imperatives of a sex-denying culture.

With respect to homosexuality, I again differ
from those who celebrate an era of sexual enlightenment. My difference is founded not only on the fact
that I believe homosexuality to be related directly to
sex-repression and to vary in prevalence according to
the degree of real sexual liberalism within a society:
it is founded also on the observation that when the
veneer of our contemporary system of defenses
against the age-old conflict over sex is stripped away,
there is to be discovered the same hostility for the invert and his way of life and the same abhorrence of
him as a person that have been traditional in Western
society. That we now employ such terms as "sick" or
"maladjusted" to the homosexual appears to me to
make little difference so far as basic attitudes and
feelings are concerned. As a matter of fact, I suggest

that precisely these designations reveal the ugly truth of our actual animus toward homosexuals and the sham of modern social-sexual pretensions; for in the current lexicon such words reflect the non-conformism of their referents—and non-conformism is the major, perhaps the only, sin of our time.

Nevertheless, it would be mistaken to deny the appearance of toleration, the mirage of easement in attitude toward the invert that characterizes the contemporary social atmosphere. As a psychological phenomenon, this attitude and the emergent pattern it bespeaks merits close attention. Because it occurs in such a basic area of life—the area of the erotic instincts and their expression—it illustrates, among other things, how flexible are the mechanisms of human defense, how social illusions are created and employed for the preservation of conservatism and even reaction under the guise of progress, and how protean are the devices available to human intelligence when it lends itself to the persistence of the conformist error.

In order to study homosexuality in the perspective proper to our day, it is necessary to define it. Within recent years, at least two definitions have been circulated widely, while a third, which appears most valid, is just beginning to command attention. The first definition is the popular one and, as such things go, is founded on a myth. It is a definition based on *overt behavior* and derives from the wide-spread habit of assigning an all-inclusive stereotype to a phenomenon that is too complex for manipulation by the average mind. According to this definition, a homosexual is a person who demonstrates publicly and, it is assumed, privately, the behavioral characteristics of the opposite sex. Thus the invert is a *pansy, nance, sissy* or *fairy*—terms which all reflect the notion that in his behavior, his manner, his activities, the individual "characteristically" and "unmistakably" apes the behavior, manner, and activities of females.

Nothing, of course, could be further from the truth. It is only the rare invert who is, in the modern idiom, "swish"; only the rare homosexual who expresses feminine traits. Apart from the fact that, as a member of a severely oppressed minority, the invert who adopts such behavior is exposing himself to ridicule, opprobrium, social and even economic ruin, this is the surest way for him to defeat his aims and fail in his perpetual search for sexual gratification. In the "gay" world it is exactly those qualities usually associated with masculinity that are found attractive and hence to be cultivated. Femininity, as such, is to be avoided in these circles, and the "queen," from whom the mass stereotype derives, is ordinarily an object of contempt among *bona fide* inverts. However, because homosexuals, too, are human and subject to the human habit of stereotype thinking, an ingredient of truth lies in the popular definition: sometimes, to reveal themselves to other homosexuals and to signalize their predispositions, inverts will adopt some

minor attribute vaguely connected with femininity—
a gesture or an affectation of speech or dress. Nevertheless, the fact remains that homosexuality and
femininity have nothing to do with each other. The
homosexual is not feminine, nor does femininity necessarily betray homosexuality.

The second definition of homosexuality is pseudo-
scientific and statistical. It is usually attributed to investigators such as Dr. Kinsey and his associates, and
has achieved wide currency because it seems to offer
a firmer grasp on a traditionally elusive subject. According to this definition—which it was certainly not
Kinsey's or anyone else's intention to make—a homosexual is an individual who has experienced contact
leading to orgasm with a member of his own sex.
Now, the Indiana researchers were exceptionally
careful to point out that their concern was solely with
describing how people act sexually. You will recall
how, in their studies of the American male, they ar-
bitrarily constructed a seven-step scale, from 0 to 6,
to describe the frequency of intrasex outlet reported
by their subjects. Examination of this scale disclosed
only that more than a third of the total male population had had some intrasex experience leading to
orgasm after the onset of adolescence. The conclusions drawn were that, at the age of thirty, among the
total white population of the United States, 83.1 percent of males rated 0—which would indicate no overt
intrasex behavior in their histories; 4.0 percent rated
1—indicating a small amount of intrasex contact; 3.4

percent rated 2; 2.1 percent rated 3—indicating an equal division between inter- and intrasex activity; 3.0 percent rated 4; 1.3 percent rated 5; and 2.6 percent rated 6—indicating exclusive intrasex outlet. In sum, the Report showed that about 6.9 percent of the male population at the age of thirty (groups 4 to 6) had had predominantly intrasex experience by that time. Reducing the age to twenty, this last figure rises to 11.2 percent.

These rather startling statistics, however, are open to misinterpretation. They do not mean that 11.2 percent of twenty-year-olds are inverts. In fact, they have nothing to do with sexual inversion and homosexuality. They merely number the occasions on which, by those ages, intrasex contact eventuating in discharge had been experienced. They take no account of such factors as availability of other sources of gratification, whether these outlets satisfied or left unsatisfied internal needs, or numerous other variables. Nevertheless, the impression they produced on the public mind was the misleading one of confusing outlet with inclination, activity with psychic tendency.

The definition of homosexuality which appears most satisfactory and which avoids the pitfalls of both the popular and the pseudo-scientific is the one on which the following discussion is based. It considers homosexuality a term applicable only to those individuals who more or less chronically feel an urgent sexual desire toward, and a sexual responsiveness to, members of their own sex, and who seek gratification of this desire predominantly with members of their own sex. Now this is a definition which covers, as far as one can see, all the available psychological, biological, and social facts available to us about homosexuality. It avoids confusing degree of fulfillment with degree of desire. It concentrates on those who harbor intrasex desires but eliminates those who obtain gratification of less specific sexuality through intrasex activity. It deals, as it should, with the main and not the exclusive desire. This definition, moreover, serves the purposes of science and speculation by excluding the bisexual while yet accounting for the existence of bisexuality. Finally, it places inversion in the perspective where it belongs; as an attitude basic to the personality wherein it resides, as a compulsion with all the urgency and driving energy that account for its persistence despite the obvious disadvantages of homosexuality as a way of life.*

Although this newer definition is successful in placing homosexuality in proper perspective, it does not explain the phenomenon nor account for its gen-

---

* This definition, of course, provides no basis for legislation. But then, after all, regarded reasonably, why should homosexuality or any other kind of sex behavior be legislated against? So long as minors are not involved, so long as force is not employed, and so long as harm is not done to the parties involved, where is the crime? The confusion, naturally, lies in the word "harm," which has finally to be interpreted in a physical sense. To give the term moral implications, as we do now, is to substantiate the charge that our society is actually sex-confused and sex-hating.

esis. This is not uncommon in the field of behavior, where definition frequently only establishes a category by ascertaining the perimeters of activity—both inner and outer—for purposes of classification or statistical manipulation. To comprehend the dynamics of inversion requires profounder insight and a more clinical point of view. Preliminary to the employment of these, however, the total sexual situation in our society requires a brief review.

Of all the activities of human beings, those connected with the exercise of the sexual apparatus have been subject to the most intensive efforts at regulation. This is a fact that requires little documentation. Historically, it is to be noted that the government of the erotic life is among the primary requisites for the establishment of human communities, and that the chief business of most if not all of the agencies that dominate the collections of men we call societies is the control of the sexual instincts. Much of the character of the successive civilizations that have risen and fallen during the ages has been determined by their basic attitudes toward sex and the organs connected therewith. These attitudes comprise the morality of the given civilization, and it is finally this morality that establishes the nature of the society, its codes of conduct, its social climate, and even its political temper.

Various societies have had varying attitudes toward sex, ranging from almost unlimited permissiveness to absolute, uncompromising dominance over the functions and apparatus involved. Our own Western Christian Civilization (Toynbee's designation), basing itself on Judaic morality, has tended toward the repressive side. It has stigmatized the erotic component of human nature as base, and has traditionally regarded everything connected with the sexual instincts with abhorrence. Perhaps even more than any previous great civilization, it can be viewed as sex-denying. As it crystallized into its present socio-political form, it increased its regulatory demands over the erotic life, constraining it in ever-narrowing channels. Prohibition after prohibition has been piled upon that aspect of existence, culminating in the present tragic crisis wherein the instincts of men are in perpetual conflict with the imperatives of their society.

The real situation regarding sex today is a kind of travesty on human nature. The drive that underwrites almost the whole of behavior and the continuation of the species is, from cradle to grave, the object of every conceivable repressive force. Although it naturally becomes manifest shortly after birth with pleasurable sensations in the organs of generation and allied erotogenic zones, any attempt to respond to such sensations is subject to censorship. During the years of bodily growth and sexual maturation, shame and guilt are attached to all forms of erotic play, while illogical, mythical fears, anxieties and punishments are made to attend the slightest exercise of the functions involved. When, at last,

at a relatively advanced age, social, religious and
legal institutions relax somewhat their prohibitive
attentions to permit the instinct and its executive organs to be utilized according to their design, they
are still allowed only a modicum of employment—
and that merely along highly specific lines. Sex, in
short, throughout the life of an individual born into
the society which you and I inhabit, is under a virtual ban, except for a brief period when, if we manage to satisfy certain requirements of time, place,
person, condition, method, manner, intention and
frequency—as well as the additional ceremonial duties imposed by law, religion, and custom—our
erotic potential may be executed.

It is in the framework of the foregoing that
homosexuality becomes understandable and its genetics clear. Given this picture of a sex-rejective, sex-
repressive society, inversion must be—and I am personally convinced after intensive study of the problem and experience with homosexuals that it is—a
pattern of sex orientation adopted by certain individuals as their solution to the conflict between the
urgency of the sexual instincts and the repressive efforts brought to bear upon sexual expression by the
reigning sex morality. The condition is, then, in essence, a reaction of non-conformity, a rebellion of
the personality that seeks to find—and discovers—a
way in which to obtain expression for the confined
erotic drives. The specific form this rebellion takes—
that of intrasex preoccupation and activity—would

appear from psychoanalytic investigation to be determined by special circumstances involving the manner in which the conflict is experienced and the time of life during which it is presented. Let it suffice here merely to mention that, in the case of those who become homosexuals, it seems that the issue of sexual conformity is raised more acutely and at an earlier period than it is with heterosexuals.

This view of homosexuality as a form of rebellion, and the homosexual as a non-conformist, cuts through much of the debris of prejudice and pretense which ordinarily interfere with intelligent discussion of the problem. It removes it to another sphere entirely, permitting us to raise and answer certain questions which are, otherwise, almost impossible to discuss dispassionately. One of these has to do with the persistent but annoying issue of inversion as an innate disposition, as an inborn deviation somehow (and unfortunately) "given" at birth and dooming the neonate forever to a life of shame. The position here maintained, of course, shows up this perhaps comforting but essentially absurd notion for what it is: a rationalization which distorts the scientific facts of heredity to avoid fixing responsibility where it belongs, *i.e.* on those sex-distorted elders who, in transmitting their distortions to the child, provoke his rebellion. Moreover, the nonconformist view of inversion settles the question of its curability or, at least, its modifiability through therapy. While the condition is doubtless a reaction-

pattern of rebellion, it is, as I shall describe presently, a negative one. In this respect it takes its place
with the neuroses, criminoses and psychoses, all of
which, as I have declared repeatedly, are destructive rather than constructive expressions of that protestant, life-affirming instinct which has set humanity at the crown of creation. When once the correct
nature of the therapeutic task in all of these instinctive aberrations is grasped—the task of somehow
transmuting negative to positive rebellion—they become amenable to treatment. Finally, and perhaps
most significantly, the proposal that homosexuality
is directly related to sex-conformance pressure offers
the hope that it can be eradicated. While homosexuals may not consider this possibility a desirable
one, it is, in the long view, a social desideratum of
no mean proportions. Presently, homosexuality is the
source of immense quantities of unhappiness and
frustration to large numbers of individuals and a
chronically irritating generator of intrahuman hostility. Its elimination would not only erase much distress but, since it can be eradicated only by a
radical alteration in the total sexual condition now obtaining in society, and since this total sexual condition is subversive of human welfare, only good can
come of the process.

There remains to be explained the adverse label
I have placed on homosexuality as a form of rebellion. To me, it seems rather obvious that, while the

refusal or (in some cases, perhaps) the inability to conform to the fundamentally antibiological sex morality traditional and increasingly enforced in Western society is commendable, the character of this revolt must be designated negative. Despite the benefits claimed for it as a way of life by its many apologists, *e.g.* Plato, it appears doubtful whether this "way" assists progress which is, after all, the final measure of value. Certainly, if we define progress in terms of the overcoming of the "triad of limitations" * pointing toward an eventual break-through into another and, presumably, higher order of being, we must reject genuine sexual inversion as a mode of behavior assisting toward such an end. This is not to say that the individual homosexual may not, in and of himself, be a valuable, contributing person whose life and work give impetus to evolution: it is merely to face the fact that as a "way" it fails to satisfy the requirements. Considered simply with regard to the underlying genetic conflict between the person and society provoked by the demand for conformity, inversion does not surmount the problem; it does not overcome the issue with any technique even approaching a progressive solution. Instead, it bypasses and actually begs the entire question. The resolution it offers to a sex-conflicted society may be —and in many cases is—individually satisfying; but

* For an exposition of this term, see "The Instinct of Rebellion," p. 140, this book.

extended beyond the given individual it loses its validity as a mode of human functioning capable of mastering the present existential dilemma.

II.

In the opening paragraphs of this discussion I stated that an unprejudiced view of the facts about homosexuality in contemporary society would reveal the presence of those traditional attitudes of hostility and contempt that have become encysted within our reigning morality. I propose now to substantiate this statement; not directly, since this would only lead to prolonged and fruitless debate over subsidiary issues and terminology, but by inference. From the major defenses erected by genuine homosexuals, individually and *en bloc,* and from the basic disposition of society revealed through its defensive processes, I think it possible to obtain a clear picture of the situa- '
tion as it really exists. First, however, let us mark out the quantitative dimensions of our problem.

The extent of homosexuality in modern society is difficult to determine. Depending upon the definition one employs, figures will vary. The popular definition, because it includes almost everyone who shows feminine behavior traits, incorporates a large group of homoerotics (about whom I shall have more to say later) and individuals with other-sex attributes which do not necessarily indicate genuine inversion. Figures derived from investigations like the Kinsey Report—with their emphasis on activity and their (unintentional) equation of inversion and intrasex contact—are similarly too high. On the other hand, estimates of some psychiatrists, psychologists, social workers and police officials who encounter largely the more obvious casualties of inversion, are likely to be too low. Homosexuals themselves, often seeking justification and anyhow inclined to commingle with their own kind, invariably overestimate their numbers; while the so-called average citizen, whose sources of information are limited, who is often even blind to the existence of inversion unless it appears in the immediate neighborhood of his family and who, in any case, finds the whole matter abhorrent, always underestimates. Defining homosexuality according to the three aspects of desire, responsiveness, and source of gratification, however, establishes natural criteria to be applied to data accruing from all of the above sources and permits a rough but more reliable estimate to be made of its prevalence. Treating the matter conservatively in this manner, the extent of genuine inversion in the United States appears to settle at a figure of roughly 4 to 6 percent of the total male population over age sixteen, or around three million individuals.

This is a large figure—although not so large as those obtained from the utilization of other definitions. In the ordinary course of events, one would legitimately expect a group of such size to exert a considerable degree of influence on the affairs of the remainder of the population. At the very least, there would be justification for supposing that, if only because of its numerical strength, it could obtain some hearing for its grievances and some support for its aspirations. However, this has not been the case with the homosexual bloc. Although it has become important and influential in an oblique and thoroughly indirect way, as we shall see, neither its grievances nor its aspirations have commanded the attention or support warranted by its size alone.

One obvious reason for the neglect of so many persons is that inverts do not comprise a well-defined minority. This is to say that the homosexual is found on all levels of society, among all ethnic groups, in every station, occupation and calling. He has one characteristic, however, that distinguishes him from everyone else, that cuts across all the interests and special features of the groups to which he belongs and establishes an abiding community with his fellows everywhere. This feature accounts for his special status in society, for the neglect he suffers *en bloc,* for the historic attitude expressed toward him.

The common aspiration of the homosexual or invert bloc is freedom to pursue a way of life dictated by special desires. Because these desires are sexual and our civilization is essentially anti-sexual, and because these desires can be gratified only in a highly particularized fashion considered inimical to its very structure, society responds to them in a manner that can only be described as uncompromisingly hostile.

The hostility that has prevented inverts from combining as a special-interest group and articulating their demands has always existed in our culture and among the socio-cultural sources of our culture. This statement remains generally true despite protestations to the contrary of apologists with an astigmatic historical purview who over-emphasize a certain brief period in Greek history, a few scattered homosexually oriented primitive cultures, and some temporary, purely local, lapses from customarily rejective attitudes toward homosexualism here and there in the past. It remains true today, beneath the defenses which I now intend to describe.

That the position of the invert in contemporary society *seems* to have altered is due, I believe, to a few quite specific defensive maneuvers adopted by (or forced upon) homosexuals for their own protection, as well as to certain similarly defensive societal devices which permit the anti-sexualism of our social order fullest expression under the mask of progressive rationality. Each of these devices, although in fact but a facet of an over-all pattern and interrelated, can be authenticated by objective observation; but as a way of clarifying those I have selected to deal with here, I have chosen a somewhat clinical and illustrative approach.

The case of Howard, a patient now under analysis with me, serves to exemplify perhaps the most
striking of all the defenses employed by inverts to
save themselves. He is a young man of twenty-eight,
highly intelligent and inordinately gifted. Before
coming to analysis he was an assistant director for a
successful Broadway musical production, an assistant
producer for another, and the director of a play that
received critical distinction but little public support.
On the eve of accepting an assignment that might
have won for him, even at his age, an enviable position in the theatre world, he suffered a severe depression, attempted suicide, and sought my help.

Howard is an invert who, in my opinion, can
serve as the prototype for the modern homosexual.
Since the age of twelve he has known about himself,
and from the time of his first awakening to the im-
perious desire that underscores his entire life he has
relentlessly pursued homosexual aims. His affairs have
been numerous. In them he has played every role the
occasions demanded and practiced every variant of
intrasex activity. Moreover, his partners have come
from all walks of life. He has held them briefly for
"one-night stands," or has participated in longer affairs. For approximately eighteen months before his
collapse he had even shared in an arrangement that
resembles marriage in the "straight" world. After the
fashion of his kind, he is always seeking, always
driven by what Cory, in an apt phrase, has called "this
omnipresent love-longing for men." Under this com-

pulsion he has frequented gay bars, attended "drags," and invaded so-called "circles" where inverts gather. His favorite method of search for a love-object, however, is "cruising," since he prefers "rough-trade." During his stay in Baltimore, for example, he haunts the streets, the parks, the railway and bus stations. In short, in his style of life and motivations, Howard is in all respects the standard invert.

But there is something about this young man that emerges from close scrutiny of him, something that breaks the image of homosexuality long sustained by society, by the straight heterosexual world. There is something about him that distinguishes him—prototype and model of inversion though he is—from homosexuals of past, less hypocritical times. I know of no better way to characterize this new quality or ingredient of inversion than to call it *sexlessness*.

Paradoxical though it may seem to ascribe such a descriptive designation to one so driven by his special sexual need that its pursuit endangers security and even life, it is nonetheless both apt and unavoidable. Howard is sexless for all purposes of outer identification. Neither you nor I, encountering him outside the gay world, would be able to identify him as an invert. Nor, for that matter, would we receive from him any clue at all as to his basic sexuality and, what is even more important, neither would we get from him an impression of *any* kind of sexuality. For Howard and his kind are sexually bland. In their public behavior, at least, they have effaced all evidences of inversion and more: they have obliterated, to an amazing degree, along with traces of inversion, most vestiges of sexuality.

Howard's asexuality is, of course, a mask. He assumes it outside of the charmed circle of "the life" (as he calls the homosexual world) and discards it with relief when he returns to the gay environment. But while he wears it, the mask serves him well. It is the perfect protection against the slings and arrows of a society which would hound him unmercifully if he should once be caught without it.

Perhaps the most interesting feature about the defense of asexuality Howard and his kind have developed—and I pause here to remark that they are the true homosexuals who are not to be confused with the queens and weight-hefting homoerotics—is that it is overdetermined. It not only hides their peculiar kind of sexuality but, as observed, *all* sexuality. This is because inverts know what the rest of us are just discovering: that we are living in a culture that is profoundly anti-sexual, mistrustful and rejective of all sex and bent upon the confinement if not the literal suppression of the sexual instinct.

The maneuver Howard has adopted has produced a superficial change in attitude toward him and inversion. By self-effacement he has disarmed society, removed himself as an ever-present threat to the standards it has subscribed to, and permitted it to resume the tranquility his predecessors disturbed. No longer does he confront the heterosexual male with

the specter of latent homosexuality he once embodied. No longer does he challenge the prevailing sexual
values of heterosexuals. Finally, no longer does he so
flagrantly, as before, evoke sexuality in a culture dedicated to its virtual elimination. All of these consequences of the invert's lately acquired sexlessness
have led to a surface change in social attitude from
uncompromising hostility to something approaching
tolerance based on the "out-of-sight, out-of-mind"
principle so typical of human psychology. But it must
not be forgotten that, underneath, all remains as it
was before.

Ralph's case affords us an opportunity to make
other and equally valid generalizations about current
social attitudes toward inversion. He is also an
analytic-patient. About four years ago, without warn-
ing, he was stricken with what appeared to be a coro-
nary attack but was later diagnosed as an hysterical
episode. On leaving the hospital, where he had been
sent for observation, his physician referred him to me.
When I first met Ralph, he impressed me as one
of the most tormented men I had ever encountered.
A prematurely balding but handsome man of about
thirty-five, his apprehension was so great that he
could hardly remain still for a moment. He sweated
from every pore, chain-smoked, and started at each
innocuous noise. Indeed, as I now recall the opening
phases of his treatment, I remember how I was forced
to curtail the length of his visits during the first six

months of therapy in order to keep him from accumulating tension to a point of danger.

Ralph's history was atypical in its details. At the
age of thirteen or fourteen he became aware of an
inexplicable difference between himself and other
boys, a difference against which he attempted to close
his mind. For the next two years or so he tried to be
like everyone else but failed miserably. To his dismay,
he found that he could not share the awakening interest of adolescence in the other sex; moreover, his
thoughts and fantasies turned in another direction. At
seventeen he virtually withdrew from all contact with
others of his age and devoted himself almost exclusively to intellectual pursuits. His seclusiveness
availed little against the tides of sexuality that swept
over him and, although he was resolute in his determination not to succumb to them, they left him guilty,
soiled and self-hating.

When Ralph was eighteen, a freshman in college,
he visited a prostitute. This was a solution born of
desperation and, as one might expect, it turned out
badly. Not only was the experience a complete fiasco,
but he emerged from it confirmed in his doubts about
himself and more than ever an object of self-loathing.
After this, he saw no other escape but through religion. Accordingly, he returned to the church he had
abandoned some years before and strove to find both
peace and forgiveness by undertaking an ascetic mode
of life. He told me later that had he had the courage
to make an absolute confession at that time and purge

himself, he would very likely have entered the priest-
hood. However, since he could not admit the facts
even to himself, much less to another party, he undertook the severe regimen he regarded as the next best
thing. By imitating, as closely as he could, the lives
of certain saints, he sought to exorcise the devil that
was tormenting him and to cleanse his mind.

Fortunately for Ralph's sanity, his body could
not sustain the fastings, chastisements and penances
he imposed on himself, and at twenty-one his health
failed. He became tubercular and was sent to a sana-
torium. On release, perhaps because the need for punishment had been satisfied through his illness, he
adopted a more sensible mode of life. He returned to
school, completed his studies with high honors, and
after meeting the requirements joined a prominent
law firm.

During the subsequent years Ralph lived an out-
wardly quiet but inwardly distressed life. He still refused to acknowledge his homosexuality, struggled
against it continuously, and tried, in every way conceivable, to disassociate himself from it. The story
of his titanic war against his nature is fascinating in
itself but must not delay us here. Suffice to say that he
lost every battle, and homosexuality remained the
chief if not the sole preoccupation of his life.

Shortly before his thirty-fourth birthday there
occurred the first of a series of events that almost destroyed Ralph and led him, finally, to the analytic
couch. One night, contrary to his usual custom, he

decided to eat out. In the restaurant he lingered at the bar over a before-dinner cocktail. A stranger engaged him in conversation and soon suggested they dine together. After dinner his companion invited Ralph to his apartment for an evening of conversation and a drink. Within an hour Ralph had been seduced into his first homosexual experience.

Following this event Ralph's conflict immediately approached a stage of crisis. He was torn as never before between desires that were now far more urgent and an almost unbearable guilt now fixed in reality. He found himself unable to forego homosexual activity, on the one hand, and unable to avoid self-disgust, shame and self-hatred on the other. He engaged in an orgy of sex *and* an orgy of guilt. Finally, in a last, desperate effort to save himself, he hit upon the solution of marriage.

As anyone could have predicted, Ralph's marriage was another failure. Instead of one person, two were now miserable. Almost at once, and despite every laudable intention and vow, he resumed the life he had tried to abandon. Affair followed affair, and these were followed by increasing distress. At home Ralph tried to sustain a fiction but could not. At last, the attempt to live in two worlds and the accumulated guilt and self-rejection became too much for him. He collapsed in the fashion I have described and asked for help.

In the analysis Ralph finally faced and acknowledged the truth about himself. He recovered his identity, lost the shame and guilt that had ruined his life so far, and began to rebuild his personality. His tension disappeared and a remarkable change overtook him, a change that can be ascribed to the release of energies bound formerly by all of the elaborate defenses he had had to maintain in order to hide from himself and preserve a fiction. Among other consequences of this profound alteration in personality was the liberation of Ralph's innate creativity, which reflected itself in an increase in his professional ability and in his home life. Another was his restoration to society as a contributing and valuable person. But in addition to these, Ralph found other and parallel benefits. One of the first projects he undertook after recognizing and exploring himself was the repair of his marriage. He discovered this to be less difficult than he had thought it would be. Confronted with the facts about her husband, his wife proved to be understanding and sympathetic. With her co-operation, a marriage that was chaotic and doomed to failure was rejuvenated on the basis of mutual respect and love. Ralph developed into a considerate husband, a more than adequate lover—although the chief source of his own satisfaction lay elsewhere—and eventually an excellent father. Finally, armed with self-knowledge and other valuable insights, he was able to participate in the activities of the life he had always longed for, this time not as a cringing, guilt-ridden, shame-covered beggar helplessly addicted to immorality and filth, but as an aware and

responsible free agent. Entering inverted society at
his level, he discovered companionship and a community of interests extending beyond the sexual, although this was, of course, the cohesive element. To
his amazement he also discovered that he was not
alone in what he had heretofore regarded as an afflic-
tion of the damned. As his familiarity with the parallel world of inversion grew, he became acquainted
with its facts. It was populated, he learned, not wholly
by social dregs and psychological cripples—although
the gay world had its expected share of them as well
as the straight world—but as much by respectable
and often influential citizens, by men of judgment,
maturity, discretion and discrimination. When he had
digested this intelligence, his liberated energies found
a new direction. He became a powerful but discrete
champion for the rights of the minority he now identified himself with and, to the degree dictated by his
position and situation, propagandized his new knowledge.

Here we must leave Ralph and return to the topic
of our concern: the true and fixed disposition of society toward homosexuals and the defenses that dis-
guise or evade them. I have presented his case in
some detail because of the inferences it permits us to
draw. Let me begin by pointing out that his circumstances, although slightly more dramatic, are altogether commonplace. Despite the sophistication we
pretend, it is still possible for a youth of today to
avoid self-knowledge as long as Ralph did and, when

it is finally forced upon him, to react in the same spectacular way. A young man (or woman), that is, although apparently deluged with sex-information and surrounded by all kinds of agencies presumably dedicated to his enlightenment and the hygiene of his mind, may live almost indefinitely in a vacuum of ignorance and solitude, fearful of exposure, condemned to tormenting and rejecting himself. This is because, on the whole, the really influential institutions of our society, the agencies that transmit its fundamental moral attitudes, have not by one iota been influenced toward sex liberalism. These social structures, agencies, institutions and establishments that do seek either the propagandizement of "enlightened" sex information or attempt to prevent (or repair) the horrors Ralph experienced, are all secondary and relatively unimportant arms of society. They bear minimal psychic weight with the individual since most of them are introduced to him *after* his psychosomatic organization has become established, *after* the damage has been done. They cannot, short of intensive psychotherapy such as Ralph underwent, markedly decrease the total burden of guilt, shame and self-loathing implanted by the prior distortions of primary cultural institutions dedicated broadly to sex-conformity and specifically to a conception of inversion as religious sin, moral debility, and wilful anti-socialism.

The exceedingly clever device of holding firmly to a fixed disposition while granting a degree of lati-

tude as regards sex to inferior and subordinate institutions is not, as it seems, a concession to liberalism or
rationality. It is a technique chosen by the agencies
that guard sex morality to maintain their dominance
over the instinctual life and behavior of the person.
It clearly reveals not only the strength and determination of these repressive forces, but also the consequences of repression in this as in other areas. As
indicated some pages back, since inversion is a reaction of non-conformity in the sexual sphere, it varies
in prevalence according to the magnitude of the pressure toward conformity. That the device we have uncovered has had to be employed shows unmistakably
that conformance pressure, hence homosexuality, is
becoming more prevalent. We can thus expect, in
future, to see this device used ever more widely; but
we should not anticipate, for the reason I have given
involving the subsidiary nature of the institutions
concerned, that fundamental attitudes will alter and
casualties like Ralph cease to occur.

Ralph's case can instruct us further, this time
relative to the myths circulated about inversion as
well as the effects upon the culture-at-large of the increasing number of homosexuals among us. After all,
a minority of about three million, not to speak of the
additional millions it necessarily implicates through
familial ties and other types of association, is not to
be ignored no matter how self-effacing it tries to be.
Somehow, in ways both direct and indirect, it must
exert an influence, either favorable to or reactive

against its characteristics and goals. This is especially true when it happens to be a minority that cuts across society and that includes, among its members, the entire range of the human spectrum. As Ralph discovered, because inversion is no respecter of class or condition, when he entered homosexual society he encountered every kind and variety of human being from every stratum of the outside world. Because he, too, had been infected by—actually, victimized by— well-known myths relating to inverts, he was surprised when he learned that among his new associates were individuals of some eminence in the community and people in position to influence opinion, taste and fashion.

As with any other condition of personality, homosexuality is to be found among persons at the very apex of the pursuits—professional, commercial, artistic and governmental—that determine social direction and climate. It would be absurd to maintain, as many have tried to do, that they owe their eminence to homosexuality. This is an unwarranted distortion of the facts, a counter-myth propagandized, very likely, chiefly by homosexuals themselves. Inverts as a group are no more intelligent, sensitive or anything else than the rest of us; these qualities are distributed among them in the same proportions as they are distributed among heterosexuals, Chinese, Baptists, Republicans or psychiatrists. However, it is true that because inversion is the theme of their lives, what they produce reflects—and reflects strongly—their inversive temperament. Unlike the World Federalist, for example, or the Congregationalist whose convictions are only incidental to his life, with the homosexual inversion is the reigning passion and dedication of existence. He therefore employs himself almost exclusively in the service of his preoccupation. The culture, then, finds itself subtly acquiring opinions, tastes and fashions that render it more cordial to the invert and his special plea. But here again it should be emphasized that under no circumstances do these influences penetrate below the crust of the culture: they affect solely the secondary agencies and manifestations, while the primary ones remain adamant according to their tradition.

Hank is not a psychoanalytic patient, but he should be; neither is he a homosexual, although he is sometimes mistaken for one by people who still cling to the outmoded notion that inversion in a male equates with femininity. I have known him for many years, and the details of his life are almost as familiar to me as the events of my own. We met during the war when he served as a corpsman in a unit I commanded. He is a salesman now and moderately successful. Every time he passes through Baltimore he calls me and we have lunch together. Some of the stories he tells about his personal adventures are amusing. A few of his experiences are relevant to our discussion.

Hank is what I would call a homoerotic rather than a homosexual. By this I mean that he engages in the various sexual activities inverts practice, prefers to associate with them, and tries to ape their behavior. Together with a large and growing number of males between adolescence and late adulthood, he affects homosexualism—or, rather, his and their conception of inversion—in dress, manners, body habits and tastes. But he fools no one, least of all genuine inverts. They know him for what he is—an effeminate male.

It may be asked why Hank and so many young men today try to throw in their lot with the homosexuals. Part of the answer, I'm sure, lies in the fact that they have been successfully propagandized by influential inverts through various media, and respond to another myth about homosexuality abroad today. This myth depicts inversion in terms of mystery, excitement and magic, and it has won for homosexuals a large following. Another reason is that being conformists, they adopt the behavior fashionable at any time; and being opportunists, they exploit what they consider to be the weakness of those in a position to offer them social or commercial advantages. If one wanted to be cruel about it, one might refer to those homoerotics who are so motivated as prostitutes who advance their selfish interests by a new wrinkle of the old casting-couch technique. Finally, it is undoubtedly true that homoerotics who, as I have indicated,

are more often than not effeminate males, seek gay
society because therein they can find the tolerance
denied them by the "jam" or straight world.

The question of why youth is succumbing to
effeminization has no place in this discussion, although it is an extremely important one. Some observers, notably psychoanalysts, believe that it is due
principally to a change, first, in the nature of the male-
female relationship and, subsequently, in the character of organization of the family unit in a direction
away from its traditional patriarchal orientation. They
point out that these twin phenomena make it difficult
if not impossible for a youth to acquire masculine
characteristics, since he is not provided in his immediate environment with a figure possessing these attributes with which he can identify. This may be,
although I doubt it. To my mind, the riddle must remain unsolved until we can get clear definitions of
masculinity and femininity—definitions that are not
subject to every vagrant shift in the surface manifestations of culture.

As a homoerotic, or effeminate male, Hank is of
course treated as if he were homosexual. What he has
experienced—not once but many times in the course
of numerous lurid adventures—can best be told in his
own words as I recall them from a recent conversation. These telling sentences, I think, reveal the very
latest social defense against homosexuality. On the
surface they seem to indicate a new deal for the invert. As we shall see, they mean anything but . . .

"The whole thing is screwy," he said. "Here we are parked off the road, sitting in the car and making gay love like crazy, when I hear this knock on the window. I see the cop and almost die. But what does he do? You'll die when I tell you! He waits for us to get dressed, then sits and talks to us like a Dutch uncle. He asks if we've ever seen a psychiatrist about our *problem*. Problem! I could have died! What are these guys—shills or something for you analysts? But it's like that all over. You make a pass at a guy in the movies or the john and right away you get a lecture on Freud. *Nobody slugs you any more!*"

Thus Hank, and thus the "new" social temper in a nut-shell—literally.

Within the last few decades the idea that homosexuality is an illness, a mental disease, an abnormality of behavior falling within the province of psychopathology, has gained broad acceptance. During the recent war, when psychiatry and clinical psychology surged to prominence, this notion took hold. Today, although many of my colleagues in these fields have abandoned that naïve view, modified it, or tend toward the conceptions I have outlined in these pages, it is clung to throughout all levels of society as an article of faith. In humanitarian terms, although mistaken, it is a "good" idea. It has benefited the invert to no small degree. He is no longer regarded by the public as a wilful criminal but as a sick criminal. As such, he is usually spared certain traditional humiliations and physical injury. Facilities for "treatment," formerly denied, are now open to him after apprehension in his guilty acts (or, more rarely, at his request following "confession"), and the services of professionals—social workers, probation officers, psychiatrists and welfare agents—are placed at his disposal. As for the average heterosexual citizen, be he police officer, storekeeper or worker, the identification of homosexualism with sickness—especially mental sickness—has a salutary effect on his feelings as well as his behavior. It offers him, in the first place, an explanation he can grasp for a phenomenon that has puzzled him. Furthermore, it confirms him in the correctness of his own behavior. Again, it rationalizes the behavior of children or relatives he may discover to be inverted. Finally, and not least in importance, it relieves him of the necessity he has always been under to respond to what is alien or abhorrent with aggression and hate. I suppose the whole matter of the pedestrian approach to homosexuality which "science" apparently confirms can be summed up in a sentence spoken long before there were such creatures as psychiatrists and psychologists, a sentence that might be written somewhere on a cave wall: "A guy must be nuts to do that!"

But there is more to this enlightened attitude than meets the eye. In fact, I fear it is not enlightened at all, but merely another maneuver, another device, to preserve the rigid sex-morality of our sex-denying society.

At the beginning of this essay I declared my conviction that non-conformity has become the major if not the only sin we know today. In a previous book, PRESCRIPTION FOR REBELLION, I devoted more than half of the volume to exploring and documenting the contention that our social order has been betrayed by the myth of adjustment to the extent that non-conformity and mental illness or disease have become synonymous. Along with other branches of knowledge, other sciences and arts, psychiatry, too, has been taken in by this myth, has, indeed, adopted it almost wholesale. Hence, the rebellious, the protestant—in short, the non-conformist—is considered sick and subject to all the arts science can muster or fashion to cure him of his "sickness." These arts are specifically designed to restore the individual to conformity—and they extend all the way from pharmicological concoctions to convulsive therapy and lobotomy. Declaring the homosexual mentally ill, therefore, brings him within the compass of this regressive view and the range of all the "therapies" devised to insure his conformity. It may masquerade as a boon to the invert and a humanitarian modification of historic prejudice and hate: it is, in fact, but another way to obtain the conformance—this time in the area of sex-behavior—our dangerously petrifying institutions demand.

To illustrate the final point I wish to make in this far from exhaustive study of homosexuality in contemporary society, I offer the following exchange of

letters between myself and a foreign party whose
anonymity must be protected. I extract these from
a voluminous correspondence over many years.

Soon after the publication in 1948 of a book ed-
ited by Albert Deutsch, I received the following letter, which is presented here in full except for necessary alterations and deletions to protect the writer's
identity:

> Dear Sir:
>
> I beg your pardon for my bad English. I am
> a writer on psychology problems and I am liv-
> ing in the Far East for my studies. I have read
> only now the SEX HABITS OF AMERICAN
> MEN and find very interesting your comment
> to the Kinsey Report and useful for a book that
> I am writing about homosexuality and its prob-
> lems.
>
> I am writing to you asking the permission
> to quote your passage "need for legal reform" for
> my book, if you do not mind.
>
> I am asking you also your opinion on an or-
> ganization of homosexuals, now organizing on
> an island of Indonesia. For what I know till
> now, I think this organization is still secret,
> for this reason I cannot give more details.
>
> Some homosexuals have created a Centre
> on that island, for all homosexuals that do not
> like to live among heterosexual people. The
> principal objects of this organization are: 1. To
> make known to the world that homosexuality is
> not a disease and not curable; 2. To have the
> possibility to organize themselves on that island
> and be free to live like their nature; 3. To make

known that male prostitutes are never homosexual—and other things like that.

I really like to know your opinions on these
three objectives and, if you give me the permission, I will forward them to the President of
that organization, who is a Chinese doctor,
graduated in the U.S.A. I have written to you
because your comments on "Sexual Behavior in
Penal Institutions" is written with an open mind
and without any prejudice. When I get to Sin-
gapore I will try to get other of your works.

Yours faithfully,

I replied to this letter, giving the author permission to quote from my article, requesting more information about the Indonesian colony, and stating
certain doubts I had about this manner of approach
through isolation to the problem of homosexuality.
Two months later, my correspondent wrote again:

Dear Doctor:
I thank you for your letter and for the permission to quote. Thank you also for the manu-
script of the magazine piece you were so kind
also to send.

About the "Movement for the Study of the
Homosexuality Problems" in Indonesia, I am
much interested in this organization but I am
contrary to some part of the policy of the Presi-
dency, and I am trying to show them also the
opinions of authorities like yourself in the matter, that, I am sure, are more like my opinions.

The President of this Movement is a Chinese doctor (now a Buddhist Priest). He is

helped by 15 people, that, except for two European medical doctors, are all people not fitted for the task (a very difficult task!). They are Indonesian Princes, a well-known Dutch writer, two English engineers, etc., all homosexuals who are trying to organize this Movement in a sort of "secret society." My idea is that this Movement must set itself the task to organize the campaign to change public opinion about Homosexuality and to give help to all people that are suffering because they think to be alone with this different instinct.

They are now organizing to print an international magazine for Homosexuals, with writing of famous authors like André Gide, etc.

The idea to organize the Centre on a far away island is to make the task easier, because it is dangerous and quite impossible to organize this Movement in a European country.

It will be very useful to have your ideas about this Movement. One member is now in Cuba. He will go later to New York and try to see you.

Yours faithfully,

When I answered this letter, I requested to be supplied with all publications of the society my correspondent wrote about, and I also asked for permission to discuss and write about the group. I expressed the opinions he asked for and, in turn, suggested that the society, when organized, might welcome, for their good and the good of inverts everywhere, a scientific study of homosexuality under such apparently ideal conditions, which I believed might be supported by American foundations and organized professional groups here and abroad. After many weeks, I received this reply:

Dear Doctor:

I thank you for your letter and I am very glad to see that your ideas are like mine about the Indonesian Organization.

I am still trying to change the idea of the President of the Homosexual World Organization (H.W.O.), but he is a Chinese and with the diplomacy of the Chinese it is difficult to succeed. He is of the opinion to keep this Organization secret, until it has a strong basis, also on the financial side. Because of this the magazine will not be printed until January 1952.

But I am authorized to meet the people interested in the Organization and to speak about it, without giving the address of the Han Temple. I am in Europe to collect material for the magazine and for the H.W.O.

When they contacted me in Asia, they asked me to help them, taking in my hands part of the work to meet people and collect opinions, suggestions, etc.

For that I am in the position to grant you permission to discuss and write about the Homosexual World Organization, but without mentioning names or places. Please speak only about the Han Temple at Nawa Sangga (South East Asia).

With André Gide's death we have lost one of our helpers and advisors.

Do you know the American writers, Mr.
A.B. and Mr. C.D.? The latter has written a little book, ——— ———, which is not very serious and not written from the medical viewpoint. This writer speaks about some homosexual clubs, like "The Order of Zahar," "The
Lodge of Athens," "Kamona Club," etc. Do you
know anything of these Clubs? Do the police
trouble them?

Your suggestion to study in a scientific way
the Indonesian Group is one of the aims of the
Organization. The first task is to change the
state of mind of this group, that have still too
many and different limitations, that make difficult the comprehension also between themselves. But I am sending a copy of your letter
to the H.W.O. and I will communicate to you
the reply.

If you know people that may help the Organization in any way, please give them my address.

Best regards,

Again I answered my faithful correspondent's
letter and, after a few months, was rewarded with another:

Dear Doctor:
I have not had the opportunity to write you
sooner, because I went to Spain and later to
Holland, where, in Amsterdam, I took part in
the First International Congress for Sexual
Equality. I have asked the President of the Conference to send you the transactions of the conference which I hope will be of use to you.

I am here giving you some information about the Han Temple: I have already written to you about the Chinese President of the H.W.O. and about the Coordinators. In 1936, with the help of some medical doctors, and two anthropologists, was started, on an island in the Gulf of Siam, an experimental homosexual colony. This was a bad experience and in 1940 the colony was closed, also because of the war in the Far East. But with the help of some German naval officers (who left the German Navy in 1939) and some Dutch people, the colony was reorganized. Astrology, religious beliefs, and modern medical discoveries have helped them not to repeat the same mistakes as before, and in 1946 the Han Temple organization was already working with the aid of people from many Countries of the world (and important people, too). With the Han Temple is now also in organization the H.W.O. with larger tasks.

The main aims of these two organizations is to promote a campaign that will change public opinion about homosexuality, and especially to give help to all people that are suffering because they do not understand themselves and are too alone in life. An international magazine will be printed in 1952. Now we have magazines in Switzerland (*Der Kreis*), in Holland (*Vriendschap*), in Denmark (*Vennen*), in Germany (*Die Freund*), in Sweden (*Forbundet Av 1948*), and many others that are not monthlies like the above noted.

Here enclosed I am sending you the translation of a folder of our invitation.

The H.W.O. is in touch with all the Asiatic (and centuries old) organizations of homosexuals

like the *Buddha-Shakti Sect* of Siam, the *High
Rooms* of Macao, the *Moon Flower Rooms* of
China, the *Sons of Mauna Loa* of Hawaii, etc.,
and aims to study the experiences of these old
organizations to show the world what homosexuality really is. We think there are too many
misguided and unhappy homosexuals who
should stop thinking of themselves as abnormal
and of others as normal. There is no norm in
sexuality. Whatever the sexual inclinations may
be, ·there is little that anyone can say or do to
change these inclinations. One is what one actually desires to be, and moralizing won't
change that one single iota. Like what is done
in Sweden, by the Swedish National League for
Sex Education, our aims must be to achieve re-
vision of all legislation in accordance with a scientific judgment of sexual tendencies, and especially, to free the homosexuals from their personality complex, and to help them to find a
special way of life that may be the way of service for the new crusade against taboos, prejudices and ignorance.

Anything you write about our organization
(naturally with the necessary discretion) will
be highly appreciated.

You may give my name and address to any-
body who wants to be in touch with the H.W.O.
for scientific reasons or because he is himself
a homosexual and desires to be helped by the
Muthu Foundation.

Faithfully yours,

Enclosed with the foregoing letter was an illus-
trated folder of invitation and its translation, a mim-
eographed press release reporting the events of the

First International Conference for Sexual Equality, and a copy of its transactions and resolutions.

The meaning of this correspondence, and quantities of similar material in my possession, is clear. It is all there: a history of hostility, contempt and oppression, the appearance of an idealistic leadership, the formation of secret societies and an underground movement, the recruitment of allies and, at last, solidification and the attempt at expression. It means, in short, that another minority is discovering itself and beginning to struggle for what it regards as its rights. As events have shown, this particular minority is finding a voice and seeking the ear of the world. Since 1952 there have been additional International Conferences for Sexual Equality and the list of organizations and publications has grown enormously. Belgium now has its Centre Cultural Belge; Denmark its Forbundet, Ganymedes Samfundet, and Internationalt Forbund for Sexual Lighed, as well as *Pan* and *Vennen;* France its Cercle de France and *Arcadie;* Germany its Gesellschaft für Menschenrechte, I.F.O. Auszer der Scheifmuhle, Verein für Humanitare Lebensgestaltung, and *Hellas, Humanitas, Der Weg, Die Gefahrten,* and *Dein Freund;* Holland its Cultur en Ontspanningscentrum, International Committee for Sex Equality, and *Vriendschap* and *Newsletter;* Norway its Det Norske Forbundet; Sweden its Friends-Club and Riksforbundet for Sexueltt Likaberattigande; Switzerland its *Der Kreis/Le Cercle;* the U.S.A. its Mattachine Society, One Incorporated, The National Association for Sexual Research, and

Newsletters, Mattachine Review, One, Gay, and *T.W.O.*

The world-wide movement to organize homo-sexuals into a clearly defined minority for the articulation of its aspirations is the most ambitious as well as the most idealistic of defenses. I am personally convinced that it is doomed to failure, although I cannot help but admire the courage of those involved. Apart from numerous other reasons, I believe this bold maneuver cannot succeed because it is based on the false assumption that the world is ready to listen to and acknowledge the special plea of the invert bloc; that society is, indeed, in the midst of a sexual revolution. To me, this is wishful thinking. It makes the serious error of mistaking social defenses *against* homosexuality for evidence of sympathy *toward* homosexuality. Both the "new understanding" of inversion as mental disease (the case of Hank) and the "tolerance" of certain subsidiary agencies of society (the case of Ralph) are hopefully misinterpreted to indicate a profound change in historic attitudes. This—as I think I have shown—is unhappily not true.

III.

The plight of the homosexual in the modern world deserves the closest study by all of us. Here is a phenomenon, affecting millions, that presents the major contentions of our era in the clearest possible terms. It relates directly to the basic issue of man versus society, of individualism versus conformity. Because it counterposes instinct to culture, it permits us to explore these issues at otherwise inaccessible depths.

Culture, as we know, is in a very real sense the maker of man, the agency through which he becomes humanized. It converts his instincts to instruments for the actualization of those purposes inherent in his structure. Such purposes are neither mystical nor incomprehensible: they unfold continuously before the species as it prepares for, and accomplishes, each successive break-through into further dimensions of existence. But culture, the maker of man, can also unmake him. It can, as it now threatens to do, unman him. This occurs when it is permitted to petrify, when its institutions and agencies lose their flexibility and harden into forms that no longer accommodate to the restless, rebellious nature of the human animal. As I intend to demonstrate in a subsequent essay,* at this point culture, now designated Society, abandons humanity. It assumes an independent existence, the character of which is the reverse of man's and opposed to his evolutionary interests. In an effort to maintain its stagnant self, it attempts to seal off and prevent the further development of human possibilities, thus writing *finis* to mankind's ever-expanding fate.

* See further, the chapter entitled "Must You Conform?"

It is the literal nightmare of most thoughtful persons today that we are rapidly approaching—or have even arrived at—the point where our society ceases to humanize man but, instead, dehumanizes him. It is this fear which has raised the hue and cry over conformity, since in conformity lies the germ of social petrifaction.

Political Creed and Character

I.

You will hear it said that communism is capturing the earth and that the last and greatest of all struggles is now in process. You will read that everywhere the underprivileged, the deprived, the toilers, are rising in their justified wrath; that they are overthrowing their masters, seizing the land and the tools of production (which are rightfully theirs anyhow) and taking the first forceful revolutionary steps toward that classless society of tomorrow wherein all men will be brothers, wherein each will give according to his abilities and receive according to his needs. You will be told that this is the wave of the future—a magnificent tidal impulse that will sweep all before it in a great and passionate cleansing to come to rest at last in a gentle sea that laps the shores of a new world, a world built on equality and liberty.

Perhaps you will believe—perhaps you are one of those who has believed—this epic fiction. Many do. With a tenacity of faith recalling the passion of Hebrew prophets and Christian martyrs, they believe. Upon the idyllic promises of this great fiction they build their lives. According to its romance they rear their children. To its vague but bright hopes they sacrifice the hours and efforts of the present. Even in the face of brutal realities the belief of these many remains unshaken. Not purges nor deportations, not concentration camps nor Arctic slavery, not betrayals nor false imprisonments nor assassinations—none of these in the slightest measure affects their belief or their loyalty . . . Why?

It is surely not the philosophy behind communism which exerts such magnetism and inspires such devotion. Philosophers have long since discredited the dogmas and propositions of systematic Marxism. By themselves, such naïve formulations could attract only the uncritical. This communism has not done: contrariwise, it has magnetized—where it has not taken whole populations by force—many of the keen-minded and sensitive among us, and has turned them into inspired instruments for the doom of one society and the realization of another.

The mystery of communism's appeal can be solved only by psychology. The question of why an outmoded and originally inadequate socio-economic system attracts men and women whose intellects would ordinarily revolt at its patent inadequacies, attracts them even after events have revealed the grim underpinning of the social order they envisage, is primarily a psychological question. Among the illuminating insights of the science which makes man, his mind and his emotions the subject of inquiry, answers can be found to this puzzling phenomenon.

To the observer who employs the psychological approach, it is at once apparent that much of the success of applied Marxism is due to its amazing ability to satisfy one of the profoundest needs of men. More than any other system that has offered itself within recent years as a vessel for human hopes and aspirations, Marxism in the guise of communism fulfills the deep compulsion we humans have to defend ourselves both against a terrifying outside environment and the raging instinctual forces within each of us; a compulsion to defend ourselves by believing, and by organizing such beliefs into those patterns that go by the name of religion.

Undeniably, men possess a need for a protective orientational framework (to paraphrase Erich Fromm) and an object for devotion. So fundamental and all-inclusive is this need that, would it not add to current confusions, it could almost be called instinctual. It is, in any event, a common tendency of human beings to construct from their deepest wishes, fears and hopes a pattern to embody them and, by devotion, to bring about their fulfillment or avoidance. Whether this need is derived, as one would suspect it must be, from that fundamental instinct of humans toward mastery of their environment and destiny in the service of evolution, is a matter that need not trouble us here. That it is a fact of human nature, however, must be recognized. No man lives who does not, in one way or another, exhibit the operation of the religious need. Indeed, no man *can* live without some kind of religion, some sustaining faith, be it only a collection of self-made illusions or a set of obsessive ideas and compulsive observances arising from his individual psychology. In the secret chambers of every heart, no matter how much the brain is directed by reason, there is still to be found a residue of that selfsame urge that led our primitive ancestors to make their weird cosmologies and our forebearers to fashion the no less weird theologies that still compete for our allegiance.

It is, furthermore, a fact of human psychology that the making of religions in obedience to the need for a faith exterior to the self follows a pattern. In his myth-making, it seems, man is an architect who works by rules that seldom if ever deviate from a rigid scheme. No matter what his habitat—jungle hut, frozen igloo, or storied masonry—a sameness can be detected in the shapes of those projections from his unconscious that become the gods of men; a strict correspondence can be observed in the fantasies and dreams he creates to become the legends of his past, his future, and his ultimate destiny; an almost tedious regularity can be found in the forms of his observances and rituals. Commonly, all over the earth and in all times, there appears to be a single schema whose outlines men employ—because they are men—when, at the behest of their need and for the sake of their lives singly or together, they construct that fabulous edifice of abstractions we call a religion.

Every prerequisite for institutionalization as a religion—a secularized religion, it is true, yet still a religion—is present in communism. Almost from the moment of its conception it has borne the hallmarks of a system of faith and worship. To its slightest details it satisfies the necessary conditions for a commanding theological system, thus lending itself effortlessly to the deepest motives of men.

The parallels between the biography of Marxism and that of any great religion are inescapable. Portents and a time of troubles—of wars, bloodshed, suffering and unrest—nourished the soil that was to become the seed-bed for a new faith. An outrider and prophet—for whom the prototype in Christianity is the Baptist John—appeared in the form of a generation of preachers finally embodied in the person of the German philosopher Hegel. Following him, there arrived the bearer of the Word, the Messiah, Karl Marx. His deification requires no documenting. Abundant evidence exists to show that the life-story of this patriarchal figure—as well as the life-histories of Lenin and Stalin, the two other members of this latter-day Trinity—demonstrates in almost fantastic detail a point-for-point correspondence with the genetics of divinity as discovered by many investigators including Lord Raglan, Otto Rank, and, more recently, the poet Robert Graves.

Nor is this all that establishes the true nature of communism to be a religion in fact. Together with all other theologies, it possesses an eschatology embracing judgment and a vision of last things—the green pastures of a proletarian heaven when the state finally withers away and a classless society of joyful equals obtains, and the black hell of social coventry to the remotest generations for the unregenerate. A hagiography, too, it can count among its attributes: what amounts, in effect, to a Calendar of Saints and a roll of canonized martyrs is an intrinsic part of its devotional appeal. An assertive body of dogma embedded in sanctified texts inscribed with the ineffable Word, a hierarchy of priests and functionaries entrusted with ceremonial rituals and protocols, a set of mysteries and initiatory rites—these, and more, eloquently complete the picture and proclaim what has been disguised as a social and political system to be, in actuality, a full-panoplied, *bona fide* religion.

To recognize this real nature of communism and to see its point-for-point correspondence with every great theological system of which we have any knowledge is to begin to solve the mystery of its magnetism for all men, especially for those without a faith, those who suffer from the unfulfillment of this deep need. A further clarification comes if we now consider when this new religion arrived on the world stage. That was at a time when each major theology was showing serious symptoms of bankruptcy and had lost its ability to "charm" men. In this period the first formulations of evolutionary biology were being spread abroad and raising hob with the beliefs and faith of all literate persons; the literary investigation and, later, what came to be called the Higher Criticism of the New and then the Old Testaments had begun to shake the convictions of the most devout; what had been the certitudes of life were being questioned not only by philosophers, scientists, and poets, but by ordinary persons who viewed a culture in transit with alarm; the institutions that had given security to men of the Western world were tottering under the impact of new ideas; finally, as the industrial revolution moved into high gear and by its mechanics displaced men in millions from what had been fixed stations in life, stability of place in society disappeared. Questing for a faith and desperate for the restoration of stability and security, men found socialism in its various aspects ready at hand, prepared on all levels to satisfy their needs and meet their despair. As Hoffer has so perceptively pointed out, all of the conditions for "true believing" were fulfilled by the crusades and movements—especially the militantly socialistic—that began in the middle of the Nineteenth Century.* They provided then, and those that remain still provide, all that the nature of man needs when his time is in flux and the order of his life is out of balance. With the religiofi-

* Eric Hoffer, *The True Believer,* Harper and Brothers, New York, 1951.

cation of Marxism and its consequent effortless transformation into the theology of communism, many
men recovered what they had lost and what they
sorely lacked: something not to live by but to die for,
increasing thus the point and poignancy of what had
become narrowed, useless, unemployed lives; an
acute sense of participation as a crusader, a feeling
of belongingness within a mass, to set against meaningless individuality; an antidote for frustration, a
framework to give life content, an object of devotion; in short, a religion.

We should not wonder at the success of communism, for so much of its success is rather that of
religion. We should instead inquire into the necessity
there is for men to make religions, particularly such
a religion as Marxism—which is, in the truest sense
of Freud's meaning, an illusion and no more than the
expression of a collective neurosis. If once the dynamics of religion-making can be understood fully,
perhaps the understanding will lead us to discover
ways to satisfy the need but spare the world the
strife and suffering that follow invariably after religion like apocalyptic horsemen. It may be that our
understanding of the dynamics involved will lead to
the discovery of some satisfying equivalent of religion, something in the nature of William James's
"moral equivalent of war." It may be—who knows?
—that we shall be led to erect something like the inventive patriots of the French Revolution sought
when they deified and worshipped Justice, Virtue,

Liberty, and an entire pantheon of ethical abstractions made concrete. In any case, the task to seek an understanding of the religious need is clear. Clear also is the question confronting us: Is it possible to supplant the old religions with a new and universal faith that will retain the appeal of our current tired theologies without succumbing to the same illusions in a form even more illusory, neurotic and destructive than they have ever been—a new and universal faith that will satisfy also reason and logic, be founded on man and not myth?

There is another and equally cogent reason why communism exerts such a tremendous appeal for men of our time, a reason particularly relevant to the case of those whom we would expect to reject it on logical and philosophical grounds. To state the matter broadly and simply, it is that communism or, what is more to the point, the Party that institutionalizes communism, is a haven for neurosis and a refuge for neurotics—actually, a great organized, systematized, ready-made neurotic defense.

Now this is not to say that all Communists are necessarily neurotic, nor that all neurotics are Communists; either of these statements would be absurd in the extreme. It is, rather, to give long overdue recognition to the fact that, in these times, the Communist parties of all countries where communism is not the official political dispensation, offer themselves to the neurotic as the temporary solution to his personal disturbance, as the framework wherein his conflicts seem to him to disappear, as the system of defense by which his real problems can be disentangled for the time being, as the solvent wherein his symptoms miraculously (if transiently) disappear.

No matter how defined technically, a neurosis is at bottom a compromise formation between the imperatives of the society in which he lives and the instinctual demands of the person. Out of the clash between the requirements of the outside and those of the inside, implemented by an individual's innate rebelliousness, a compromise is born. The unstable treaty that thus results is the neurosis, essentially nothing more than a technique, a device, for adjustment, for peace. This "peace," be it ever so incomprehensible to the beholder, so apparently disquieting and even disabling to the person involved, is nevertheless the means he has selected to live a less distressed life between the hammer of the culture and the anvil of his personality.

The major attractiveness of the Party is that within its confines—as constrictive as these may be—the peace for which the tortured neurotic seeks is available. Here, tailor-made, as it were, is a cloak for the perplexed and driven who has been straining to no purpose or avail against the world, against a society that has been threatening him, against an order and way of life he cannot abide. To obey his instinct and to rebel against his culture or that part of it which intimidates him is to court disaster; to find a positive way of rebellion is beyond him. Toward the Party, then, he flings himself with abandon, seeking surcease from his conflicts. The tragedy for him, of course, is that the easement he sought is not to be found in the arms of the cold monolith he has so eagerly embraced: the tragedy for us is that we have lost—sometimes only for a while, but often forever—a potentially positive rebel whose verve could have fed the power-sources of evolutionary progress had we the courage and sense to organize a better society, a society in which the rebel-nature of the individual is not twisted into the distortions of neurosis by pressures to conform.

Most of the true believers who enter the Communist parties of the world do so because it is to them mainly a way of making an adjustment to that world. Substituting the Party for their neurosis, in each case the Party becomes an expression of their neurosis. It becomes, in short, the symptom of their inner distress and dis-ease; and like any other neurotic symptom or complex of symptoms, it performs a definite and valuable service for those who adopt it. The essence of this service lies in its adjustment value.

Our understanding of this seeming paradox may be aided by the following consideration. Here are individuals shocked by and incapable of handling their urgent needs, their secret desires, their intimate trends of personality to which the world has said a resounding NO!—and who are in chronic, desperate

search for a way both to express and satisfy these
inner promptings without alienating themselves completely from society. Within the Party this can be
done: their negative, unwholesome, destructive rebellion herein is at once liberated *and* held in check,
condoned *and* contained; and all of this without the
usual exaction of guilt under an illusion of positive,
vigorous, progressive protest.

Can we wonder further at the seductiveness of
that organization that has come to be known everywhere as *the* Party? Add to the foregoing the satisfactions such allegiance gives to the religious need which
has, in our time, nowhere to go, and the wonder is not
why so many seize upon the Communist faith, but
that many more do not.

It takes, of course, a total surrender to adhere to
the Party and to submit to its discipline, but for the
distraught neurotic even the abandonment of his
birthright of individuality and personal freedom is
not ordinarily a price too expensive to pay for the relief thus obtained. Great comfort and ease are to be
found in the adjustment the all-consuming Party offers. In addition, its rationalizations are particularly
attractive to those who have lived in self-disgust. By
a curious maneuver of logic that converts what is
really a giving-in and a giving-up of the struggle to
a delusion of special election, and by the additional
indulgence in the further delusion of messianic service to humanity, all doubts are temporarily stilled and

the real selfishness of the dedication is lost in a gran-
diose fantasy of self-less altruism.

It would be absurd to generalize dogmatically
about the psychic structure of all Party members, but
it would be even more absurd to turn a deaf ear to
data about them that have been accumulating in recent years. Who are these people who are drawn to
the Party? More pointedly—what are they?

In the United States, at least, and very likely
everywhere, most Party members are the sons and
daughters of middle-class parents or of parents whom
the great depressions, the wars and crises of the internal economics of this and other countries have displaced. In the former case, it has been their middle-
class morality, with all that it entails, against which
the children have become mutinous: in the latter
case, there has been an identification with the frustration and embitterment of the parents, which disaffection has been adopted by the children. In all cases,
however, they are the products of conflict between
conformity and protest, rendered both childish and
neurotic in psychological make-up and lacking the
personal resourcefulness and the outside guidance to
convert their instinctive rebelliousness to positive and
creative outcome. Full of dependent longings which
their parents could not or would not satisfy, consequently driven by childhood fears of rejection and
abandonment, internally torn by strong tides of ha-

tred, aggression and hostility, lonely, their horizons limited and their egoistic dreams doomed to frustration, they need—and find in the Party—a harnessing agent to prevent their destructive impulses from spilling over into action.

Intimate study of the mental make-up of the average Communist leads to the conclusion that, in most cases, he joins the Party because it offers him a defense against his neurosis and actually replaces it. What seems to have escaped notice, however, is the fact that in becoming the analogue of the neurosis, the Party acts as a safeguard against indulgence in behavior that might otherwise result from the extremes of pressure under which a person so constituted finds himself. In other words, the function the Party assumes for most of its rank-and-file members is the function of withholding destructive impulses from direct expression.*

There is, however, another group of Communists to whom these remarks do not apply. This is the group from which the leaders of the Party are drawn, the inner cadre that comprises the hard core of the movement. In psychic structure these true believers partake of the mental complexion of a type that is to be found predominantly among Fascist rather than Communist parties. Subsequently, we shall see that

---

* The reader is reminded that, throughout this discussion, except where indicated, we are dealing with the Party *before* it becomes—if, as in the Soviet Union, etc., it ever does—the official Party of the State. As we shall see, the situation is radically different once it achieves power.

the psychology of the Fascist is quite different from that of the Communist. Anticipating that discussion somewhat, it may be relevant to point out here that a major distinction between the Communist and the Fascist appears to be that the latter, far from seeking the containment of his destructive impulses, looks for an instrument through which they can be expressed; and as the Communist rank-and-filer finds his desire for *withholding* met by the Party, so the Fascist discovers his need for acting out and *expressing* destruction fulfilled by the movement he joins. The Fascist, therefore, is not to be described as a neurotic person, for this urge toward the acting-out of his internal distress stamps him rather as a psychopath; as an individual, that is, who tends to evidence his conflicts and satisfy his instinctual needs not by suffering or by symptoms, but by direct outward show, usually a "show of violence."

It is characteristic of all movements and crusades that the psychopathic element rises to the top. So it is with the Party. Its hard core, its small and relatively stable inner circle, is made up of men who show the typical developmental course and the resulting psychic structure of the psychopathic personality type. For them the Party is certainly not (as it is for the rank-and-filer) an organized defense against the realization of the secret self that resides within each of us, but an instrument by which their secret selves can be realized. The uses to which they put the Party are quite different from those for which the common member employs it. To them it is a tool; to the others a refuge. Why they elect to grace a Communist rather than a Fascist party is a question of little importance here and one that has been answered already by Hoffer and others. What is important for us to note, however, is that it is due to them that any practical distinctions between these contending factions sooner or later become either negligible or non-existent, even though in origin, ideology or methodology they may appear to be dissimilar. Because of the undifferentiated character of the leadership which eventually imposes itself upon both groups, and because the invariable mechanics of such movements result in a gradual sloughing off of all types but the psychopathic—by the process to be described below—what at one time may have been valid differences between Communist and Fascist organizations tend to disappear in practice and to be obliterated finally when and if either achieves the power it seeks.

These statements are readily verified if one takes the trouble to examine the facts dispassionately. Of particular relevance are two statistical items: the first of these is the rapid turnover of membership in all Communist parties as contrasted with a far slower rate in Fascist organizations; the second is a marked difference in what may be called the fate or destiny of the rank-and-filers of each of these groups.

It is a matter of common knowledge that the hard core of the Party remains relatively fixed everywhere while the membership is in constant motion, changing always as recruits replace deserters in a seemingly endless chain. This, however, is not to be observed in parties of the Fascist dispensation. Contrariwise, they tend (if they survive at all) toward rapid increment in membership once they have passed through crucial formative stages, and the rate of desertion they show is minimal compared to that from the Party. It is also true that "once a Fascist, always a Fascist," whereas the same does not seem to hold in the case of the Communist. Fascists, that is to say, rarely leave the charmed circle of fascism: it is characteristic of them to drift endlessly from one Fascist "party" to another as opportunities for the exercise of their needs are created by the generation of one after another of such parties. On the contrary, Communists behave quite otherwise. When they desert, it is unusual for them to join another political party. If they do not relinquish all activity of a like nature and retire to cultivate their personal concerns, they show up in the ranks of the more highly organized religions or among cults that cater to the occult and the metaphysical.

These two well-documented observations speak volumes to the psychologist. To him they indicate that the psychic structure of the Communist is of an altogether different nature from that of his opposite number, the Fascist, and that the purpose for which each joins his movement (what the movement does for him, that is) differs.* It becomes apparent to him

* Eric Hoffer, among others, makes a special point of the essential similarity of both factions and the interchangeability of their membership. He appears to think that both parties,

that the rapid and continuous turnover in the membership rolls of the Party is due to the fact that, at any given time, the Party contains largely those neurotics who can find their havens within it precisely at that time. Whatever the role the Party may be playing at the moment, whatever line or policy it may be following for that period, whatever character it may have in that interval, it lends itself primarily only to a certain group of neurotics. Temporarily relieved of their conflicts, only for the *now* do they find their adjustment. And a most unstable and tenuous adjustment it is; for not only is the neurotic himself always pre-

---

originally and later, offer the same things to their followers. Obviously, I do not wholly agree. I believe that the parties are actually different in ideology and structure. I think the evidence shows that, until a certain point in its development— a point proximate to the place where it comes within reach of power, or in the stages immediately preceding the seizure of power, and, of course, when it is in power (obtained for it primarily by the psychopathic element)—the Communist Party serves chiefly the neurotics who want their aggressions held in check, whereas the Fascist parties offer the psychopaths a vehicle for continuous and uncontained expression of their aggressions in act. I have also observed it to be more likely the case that Communists who become Fascists—or vice versa —before either party comes close to or achieves power, were misfits in the party of their original allegiance; in the one instance, neurotics among psychopaths; in the other, psychopaths among neurotics. On this basis there may be and is considerable interchange as mistakes are corrected. It is my further understanding, as I have indicated, that the absolute and terminal temper of both parties is psychopathic, that their final success is due to their appeal to the latent psychopathy in the mass, that they get and hold power by the progressive uncovering of the latent psychopathy in all of us. For a fuller expression of these views, see my PRESCRIPTION FOR REBELLION (Rinehart, 1952).

pared to discard one expedient "solution" to his distress for another that appears to promise safer and snugger anchorage for his neurosis, but the Party too, by its very nature and structure in the stages while it seeks power, is variable, inconstant and ever-changing. Therefore, in practice it is to be observed that, as policy shifts and changes, the Party is deserted and even betrayed by its personnel at a startlingly rapid rate.

You will be (and are) told that the real reason for the abandonment of the Party by its members (Recall the mass defections at the time of the signing of the Nazi-Soviet Pact, during the Russo-Finnish War, et cetera) is to be explained differently. The individuals involved tell us that they could not, in the given instance, subscribe to the policy-change intellectually, that they disagreed on rational grounds with the new direction implicit in the change of line, even (in some cases) that they were offended on humanitarian grounds by a specific directive for an ideological or actional alteration. From the side of the Party it is usually given out that the deserters were "unstable elements" in the first place, and chronic vascillators to boot, whose ideological and personal instability were known already to the higher-ups. But none of these reasons, nor the many others ordinarily employed to explain the transience of membership in the Party, are more than rationalizations. The truth is that the shift somehow, in each case, endangered the adjustment the individual deserter had until then found within the Party, and he was now threatened

with a resurgence of his neurosis. Having joined the
Party primarily to satisfy certain needs and to quiet
certain symptoms, when the Party fails him by failing
to fulfill its defensive role, he can do nothing but quit
and look elsewhere.

These speculations as to the psychology of the
true believer of Communist persuasion lead to an interesting conclusion about a matter that has intrigued
many of us. Commentators and observers have always
assumed—and have led the rest of us to believe—that
the accusations of treason leveled against certain
prominent Communists during the Moscow Trials of
1937 in the Soviet Union, the purges in Hungary and
Rumania, and the recent dramatic series of court-
room spectacles in Czechoslovakia, were trumped-up
and false. The foregoing psychological findings, however, would lead us to suspect otherwise. Indeed, if
what has been said throughout this essay has validity,
the conclusion must be that the men and women who
stood trial and then suffered sentences of exile, imprisonment or death were, in almost every case,
guilty. They may not, of course, have been guilty of
the specific and usually fantastic crimes that appeared
on the docket of indictment—and it goes without
saying that their "confessions" and *mea culpas* were
very likely induced by sometimes drastic means; but
of their guilt as to treason against the state and conspiracy there does not seem to be room for a shred
of doubt. For there is this phenomenon to be observed
regularly when, in any given instance, the Party

finally achieves power (*vide,* the countries behind
the Iron Curtain and Communist China): at once,
and as a natural corollary of power, the Party changes
its character. It can no longer—because it is now operated by the psychopathic core and in its career toward power has replaced most of its membership
with personalities in structure predominantly psychopathic—it can no longer perform its precious function
of defense even for those relatively "hardy" neurotics
who have survived until then and still remain with it.
Therefore, at this juncture, they are forced to abandon what has been for them a protecting shelter. If
they can (and usually they cannot) some resign; but
the rest are exposed to the torment of their neuroses.
They are then driven to seek for, and eventually they
discover, a new but now underground harbor for their
threatened selves. Once more, in the oppositional
cults and cells into which their psychological needs
drive them, they find an illusion of surcease. Toward
the Party which formerly commanded their allegiance, then, and toward the State which the Party
now embodies, they are patently guilty.

II.

Under the rubble of Berlin there lies the corpse
of one who embodied in his person the forces that can
and very likely will undo our civilization. We can

only despair that the chancellery that collapsed on him was made of mere stone, that it could entomb only his flesh and not the spirit he represented—not the plague of which he was but a germ. For the menace of world-wide social psychopathy did not die with Adolf Hitler: indeed, it hardly suffered even a temporary setback with the fall of his vaunted "Thousand Year Reich." Our antagonist is merely resting—where he is not already marching—resting and waiting to be aroused from the torpor of inaction by the galvanic slogans of the Leader he has been expecting almost since the day he drew his first breath.

The public at large knows little and cares less about the kind of persons we psychologists call psychopaths. If the average citizen ever comes across the term in his reading, he ordinarily imagines raving madmen and consigns them to the care of hospital psychiatrists. Or, if the citizen is a little more sophisticated, he thinks in terms of crime and daring escapades, and relegates the perpetrators to the province of the police. He does not know—he has not been told—that the psychopath is the enemy of his life, the adversary of his welfare. He does not know—he has not been told—that the psychopath is the harbinger of social and political distress, the carrier of a plague of wars, revolutions, and convulsions of social unrest.

To combat the rising tide of psychopathy must become a task to which citizens of a democratic society have to dedicate themselves if they want their civilization to continue. One of the highest missions a man of our culture can have is this: to identify the psychopathic antagonist and to struggle against the conditions that produce him. Let us try, therefore, in the following paragraphs, to draw a profile of our enemy. And let us study this picture carefully: observe him closely as we would under a microscope a virus of pestilence. We will discover what we have hidden from ourselves for so long: that he is composed of elements that are in all of us; that he thus holds the key to the arousal of what is base in us and our neighbors; and that he uses this key to unlock the foulest part of our natures. And it may be that from this portrait we will learn what is our business: to prevent him from raising his provocative voice again; to keep him from spreading his primitive, intoxicating philosophy of force; to restrain him from distributing his poison that sets one man against another.

There walk among us men and women who are in but not of our world. As a group, they suffer from a disorder of the total personality that absolutely unsuits them for social living. As individuals, it has been observed many times that they are driven by often irresistible pressures to move against the main stream of life, to place themselves by their deeds outside the pale of the community, to be in perpetual conflict with the world about them. Spurred to wild and extravagant behavior by clamoring needs, by insistent demands of their nature, they are best described as chronic and cause-seeking rebels whose essential aggressivity can be aroused with minimal effort. For this reason, they are the darlings of the demagogues, the delight of the fish-market Demosthenes and the street-corner Catalines.

Behavior experts designate people of this kind "psychopaths" or "psychopathic personalities." By this term is meant individuals distorted in their reactions to the community and to other men. For them, the rules of conduct and the laws that govern the relations of humans—rules and laws won painfully over the millennia of man's tenantcy of Earth—do not exist. All those qualities which ordinary, non-psychopathic people strive to obtain, all the values that give life meaning, are foreign to the psychopath. From this derives his menace to the security of everyone.

We all know who the psychopaths are, although we do not always give them that label. Literally, they wear their symptoms on their sleeves. Often the sign by which they betray themselves is crime, crime of an explosive, impulsive, reckless type. Sometimes the sign is ruthlessness in dealing with others socially, even commercially. In these days, however, the sign is more frequently hate, bigotry, intolerance, and violence expressed politically for the purpose of self-satisfaction, self-aggrandizement and power.

Until fairly recently, while behavior scientists were able to describe the psychopath, they could not account for his genesis nor for the curious phenomenon of his being. As a matter of fact, they were tempted—and some still are—to think of him as a biological anomaly, an atavism, a throwback to primitive times. And, indeed, there are grounds for this view, or at least many good reasons why such a point of view persists. When you come to know him in all his violence, in all his contempt for the basic tenets of communal living, the psychopath is not unlike the brutes of prehistory with their vicious selfishness, with their callous disregard for the rights and feelings of others.

After years of patient research with the tools of psychological dissection fashioned by Freud and his followers, we now know the mechanics of psychopathic behavior and can reconstruct the dynamics of its manifestation both in individuals and societies. We have learned that it is not an abrupt rebirth of the past, not a sudden, unaccountable upthrust of nature from our racial history. Instead, we have come to understand the condition as a patterned response to life—or better, a life pattern—inexorably fashioned almost from birth and goaded into spasmodic expression in persons and groups by psychic pressures released when a society fails to build the kind of social order men require for creative, harmonious living.

It is in infancy that the foundations of individual psychopathy rest, and it is an infantile pattern that persists with the psychopath to the end of his days. In that dim time, because he was mismanaged by his parents or guardians, his sense of self, his ego, was damaged; and no technique of repair short of a radical therapy designed to undo the damage and remake that ego can correct the primary fault. For most psychopaths the initial hurt to the ego grows out of the erotic triangle: mother, child, father. Because, for numerous reasons, a proper and proportionate image of the father is not absorbed, all that in later life stems from the father in Western culture—authority, precept, custom, morality—is fated to be rejected with hate. This hatred, moreover, because it is bound up with fear, with apprehension of bodily injury of the most intimate kind—ordinarily, harm to the procreative organs—takes a violently aggressive, outgoing form. Expecting to be punished for his hatred, the psychopath forever lashes out at his environment with a recognizable indifference for where or on whom his blows fall. And, fatefully, with this manner of behavior, he sets up a psychic chain from which only death can free him. With each aggression he increases his guilt, hence his further expectation of punishment; so we find him acting always with more aggression, more violence, and acquiring only more guilt.

But it is not—as it has so often been given out by writers who know the psychopath only superficially —it is not alone in respect of their fathers that these people are distorted. In most instances the mothers (or their substitutes) contribute equally to the making of this human deviate. Characteristically, when we trace the psychopathic story to its beginnings, we learn of the maternal onus for the defective ego.

Briefly, we find, in case after case, a tale of seduction on the mother's part; not necessarily a sexual seduction, but rather an emotional binding of the child to the mother, a desperate overindulgence that arises from her anxiety, a frantic possessiveness of the offspring that prevents him from developing a real and independent self. In the face of this, his ego does not ever have its normal chance to split off from that of the mother, and there comes about a co-extensiveness of the self first with the all-providing, never-denying maternal ego, then with the entire world from which the immediate gratification of need is expected. When, in the course of events, as it must happen, these needs are not at once satisfied, there supervenes hatred for those who deny, and violent wrenching of what is wanted from wherever it can be obtained.

The borderless ego developed by the psychopath as a consequence of maternal seduction leaves him with two characteristics every observer has noted: an inability to grasp the distinction between "mine and thine"—hence his penchant for appropriating what is not his and a completely defective sense of property—and a megalomanic conception of self, a total self-ishness, that causes him to behave as if he alone counts in the world, as if he is the tot of Destiny and her chief concern. He is thus unsuited for life in a world that will not give him everything he wants when he wants it, unsuited for life in a world that will not endlessly and unprotestingly feed his grandiosity.

Another characteristic of the psychopathic per-

son is his incapacity for love, both for the receiving
and the giving of it. Added to the peculiar ego con-
struction sketched above, in his development it has
come about that the civilized uses of love in both the
sexual and affectional senses are alien to his special
nature. In the fantastic drama of his infancy, the
male parent—or whomever it may have been who
stood in the way of his complete possession of the
maternal figure—appeared to his single-purposed
perception to forbid, to stand in the way of, the mother's demonstrations of affection and his own search
for continuous gratification. For him, love became
incest, and in his unconscious the racial taboo was
stirred, evoking inadmissible images with horrible,
race-derived punishments. To avoid such consequences, and yet to satisfy ordinary needs, it hence-
forth became necessary for him to select erotic ob-
jects, and to do erotic deeds, as far as possible removed from the cherished but forbidden maternal
image. So, in the psychopath, both male and female,
the drive becomes adventitious, diffuse, non-selective,
and always non-satisfying. It expresses itself mainly
by perversions to avoid guilt, but it only succeeds by
this kind of expression in achieving more guilt. The
sex act itself, as he performs it, is no more than a
primitive, purely biological outburst, usually accomplished without the preliminaries our culture requires.
Often, in the attempt to avoid the incest prohibition,
it takes a homosexual form; but it is done, even here,
with an object of convenience rather than choice, and

consummated at white heat with violence and contempt for the other person.

Added to the features so far mentioned, the psychopath reveals many others which need not be dealt with here since they are of primarily clinical interest. What needs to be emphasized, however, is the persistence into adult life of the utter infantilism which the psychopathic personality discloses. In boldest relief stands the single major criterion of immaturity—the inability to await the satisfaction of desire and need with time. Like children, these persons cannot wait: they must have what they want in the moment of their want. Their behavior, then, necessarily violates the arduously tested requirements of civilized adult living, neglecting, as it does, the intermediary stages between desire and satisfaction and so leading to trespasses of law and decency. Here emerges the crux of the matter, the core of the problem created by the presence in society of such deviates: psychopathy is a social disease; its effects—unlike those of most other mental disorders and aberrations—are directed outwards, away from the self, and upon individuals and groups which, because they are essentially social and decent, represent what the psychopath most fears, most hates.

If psychopathy were a condition of behavior and mind confined to a few scattered individuals, the entire matter could be left for the attention of medical psychologists, the keepers of prisons, and the attendants of private and state psychiatric institutions. But it is not: it is a world-wide disorder, affecting huge segments of the population of the globe, and spreading like some malignant growth within the body of human society. This is because all of us are somewhat psychopathic. What saves some of us from the expression of our psychopathy is either a fortuitous combination of circumstances that keeps us relatively normal, or the less fortunate fact that the adjustments we make are of a different order—neurosis, insanity, or physical illness. In many of us the psychopathy is never evoked, or we are happily able to erect defenses against clamorous infantile urges. Most of the situations we encounter do not threaten us with a reawakening of the anxiety attached to the conflict between infantile wish and prohibition, hence they do not spill over into catastrophic act. Nor—and here is the point—nor do all of us live in the kinds of society which thrust upon us situations reminiscent of infantile scenes we have repressed, of infantile hurts and frustrations.

When psychopathy becomes—as it has in the past and threatens to in the future—a matter no longer of individuals but of groups, nations, peoples, and continents, its political significance becomes manifest.

The latent psychopathy of the human race, that core of bitterness and hate which in the best of us is unresolved, can be awakened first as a result of deprivation and prolonged denial of basic wants. What is initially required is a threat to security, a disinheritance, or a dispossession. These serve to mobilize the ancient fears, penetrating to recesses of the personality where lie the pains and disappointments of the first decade of life.

The second requisite for the arousal and spread of this virulent infection is, of course, a Leader, who is necessarily himself a psychopath, a person touched with the same madness. As the epitome of frustration and bitterness, he it is who translates into slogans the disaffection of the masses. Such touchstones of negative rebellion are flaming affirmations of their hurts and disappointments. They appeal directly and forcefully to the primitive, unsatisfied hungers of infancy: they promise retribution and vengeance a thousand-fold in a world that replaces their dreams, a world where one is honored, even commended, for the very things one has wanted to do all along but has not done for fear of punishment: they promise fulfillment of the secret wish to rule again as one once ruled through the bars of the cradle. Such slogans are by now so familiar that repetition here is pointless: their themes run the brief gamut from the Caesarian "bread and circuses" to the foul incoherencies of the *Horst Wessel Lied.*

Only a brief backward glance is required to perceive the truth of these propositions. An examination of such phenomena as the spread of fascism abroad and the growth in our own country of the gutter-führered, be-shirted and bedecked (note the infantilism of the trappings!) movements of prejudice and

regionalism give eloquent supporting testimony. Be
it observed how in all of these it was (and is) the
precariously balanced middle class and its children
who were so readily recruited into the ranks of bigotry and hatred. The hold which fascism obtained
on the Italians, the Germans and others was through
the dispossessed and disinherited, the betrayed who
had fallen from the lower rungs of the economic lad-
der. These became the lumpen-proletariat, the hopeless whose petition for social justice was in reality a
request for reinstatement in a place they considered
theirs by right. They were the ones who had been
scorched by the First World War and the subsequent
inflation and hunger, being thrust together within a
psychological cage of insecurity, anxiety, and fear.
So, too, it was in our South as a result of depression
and the minute, tentative advances into economic
rivalry of the Negro; and, again, in the industrial
North under the specter of unemployment and insuffi-
ciency.

In its individual form psychopathy is an episodic
type of disorder. The person so constructed does not
behave in an unruly, destructive fashion all of the
time. It is as if he pauses between onslaughts against
the environment to gain fresh strength, meanwhile
accumulating tensions to the blowing-off point. On
the world-wide scale the same thing applies. That
we are now in a state of relative quiescence is without significance. But it is at this point that those of

us who see and understand the menace can and must act.

Psychopathy is nurtured in a bed of despair, matures in a soil of frustration, and produces its malodorous blossoms in a climate of repression and conformity. When, in the course of its development, a society reaches a static stage and becomes anorganic, fixed, set in a pattern that does not permit its members the satisfaction of natural and acquired aggressivity and scope for their rebellious inclinations, the danger point is reached. But so long as frontiers remain, so long as there are places and areas where compulsions can be worked off and individuality asserted, the exploding tensions do not turn inward. Frontiers, therefore, both physical or psychological, are a necessary part of a healthy society. As these disappear, they must be replaced and adequate substitutes for them provided.

When William James wrote his masterly "The Moral Equivalent of War," he merely affirmed what every psychologist has learned and what every government should know. In this essay he stated his belief that it is possible to exhaust the destructive urges of humans in the fight against Nature, and in this manner to preserve the best of the martial spirit while avoiding wholesale its evil consequences. Because the world has changed so radically, the word "Nature" now demands a broader interpretation; but the principle remains the same. Aggressive man, whether he be openly infractious because of an essentially psychopathic make-up, or touched but lightly with this distortion, cannot long endure imprisonment, cannot long live within a social stockade. We have been shown repeatedly by history that where insecurity and anxiety have no outlets (as in restrictive political frameworks), where a society is walled in and escape-valves for disaffection are lacking, mass tensions, pieced together from the disparate elements of individual psychopathy, either burst their bounds and rush headlong against the barriers, spilling over into aggressive wars; or they are turned back and in upon themselves and are expressed as civil disturbances, a major increase in crime—which is chronic civil war—and intergroup strife.

In the permissive atmosphere of true democracy the horizons are never limited, the boundaries never set. So long as men can work out their piled-up tensions by socially channelized aggression the population as a whole is not overwhelmed by psychopathic impulses. There may be miniscule movements and regional outcroppings of anti-social aggressiveness, and psychopathically motivated crime may continue, but the large mass remains relatively unaffected. With the spread of education—a pillar of democracy—another realm for the expression of healthy aggression is thrown open, and the Nature of which James wrote expands to include a universe of idea and invention to be attacked vigorously. Moreover, inherent in the democratic formula is the acceptance of the principle that a certain amount of positive rebellion and a spirit of vigorous protest are essential to its realization, and that the expression within limits of individuality to satisfy compelling personal needs is a healthy technique for the retention of social equilibrium.

Strangely enough, all of the foregoing is substantiated by the scientific observation that the predominant form and manifestation of distress in societies which aim toward democracy is not psychopathy but neurosis. Neurosis, as Karl Menninger and many others following Freud have shown, is *self*-destructive. The aggressivity is pointed inward upon the self as object, the frustrations and thwartings encountered in life exert upon the individual sufferer or, less often, are worked out upon those who stand in intimate relation to him. The neurotic suffers out his perplexities and problems, while the psychopath acts them out. Where, in a relatively free society, an individual fails, or where his relationships in the world deteriorate, he tends to look within himself for the fault or error; he grows hostile toward himself and expresses the hostility by symptoms and behavior hurtful to *him*. In the unelastic, limited social atmosphere elsewhere, the target is the not-self or the outside world. Recall in this connection the celebrated *weltschmerz* of the pre-Nazi German and contrast this self-castigating sufferer with his truncheon-wielding offspring. Recall also—and think about it carefully—that the Soviet medical authorities have boasted of the strikingly few cases of neuroses precipitated by war among their soldiery as compared with the high neurotic incidence in the American and British armies. To the psychologist this is a significant if minor indication of the essentially psychopathic nature of Soviet society and its leadership, a nature acquired as it approached power and crystallized when it obtained success.

While psychiatrists and psychologists are not prepared to state categorically that psychopathic personalities are born with a special kind of biology (there is some evidence that this may be the case), they *are* prepared to declare that the environment touches off, or precipitates, psychopathic behavior. These precipitants are liberally provided by the economic and social climate of our civilization. Were they not present, much of crime and social unrest in the democracies would disappear, while the potential for conflict in other countries would fall. To reiterate them would only be to recount the inadequacies and again expose the ulcerating sores of our culture. They include the abomination of the slum, underprivilege, intolerance and the whole familiar, weary list of social and economic evils. In these are the frustrations and thwartings, the resentments and disappointments that make for the climate of conflict and provide another limb for the million-footed golem that knows only how to destroy. They are the breeders of the essential criminal who bands with his fellows in a confraternity of vengeance cemented by allegiance to the cherished Leader. So, until we systematically eliminate them—these social and economic seedbeds of psychopathy—we will continue to nourish the instrument of our destruction.

III.

It has become fashionable to maintain that communism and fascism are essentially alike, that there are no real distinctions to be drawn between these contending forces. This broad statement overlooks many of the relevant facts. The appearance of similarity is a function of the phenomenon—pointed out previously—that *the entire complexion of communism changes in the phase when it actively contends for power.* It is at this point that the psychopathic core of the given Party reveals itself and induces those radical transformations which wipe out what were, until then, valid differences. But until the moment that marks the beginning of actual, open struggle for power, there exist many clear divergencies between the two systems. While this is not the place to itemize the differences, it should be pointed out that they are to be found among the philosophical propositions on which each system is (presumably) based, in their methods, in the structure of their units, and in their stated goals. Due to these differences— always with the reservation that we are speaking here of the period we have called *antecedent*—each attracts a different kind of personality.

In the same way that the Communist parties in the antecedent phase attract the religion-starved and the neurotic, so the Fascist parties tend to draw to themselves the rejected, displaced and psychopathic. These latter are, to all intents and purposes, egoless. Bursting with tensions they cannot long control nor convert into symptoms (for technical reasons relating to structural complexities of their peculiar personality disorder), they find in the given Fascist party an extraordinarily suitable vehicle for the expression of their internal stress. The demand of fascism that they become human robots, that they conform to a certain physical and ideological discipline, that they become automatically obedient cogs in a giant social mechanism—this demand calls for no sacrifice of individuality, no psychic surrender of self-hood, on their parts, for they are already so constructed that they have no real, personal selves to give up; it is, curiously, only by a merger with the group mind, by participation in the group ego, that they discover a sense of self. Purposeless, unsatisfied, discontent and hollowed inside by a pervasive awareness of their rejection, they seek and find in the uncompromisingly rigid fascistic organization purpose, satisfaction, a kind of contentment and a replacement for internal emptiness. The identification they make with a Leader is not only instinct-satisfying in the profoundest sense in which all men yearn for an omniscient Father, nor is it only gratifying in the religious sense applicable to the species at large; but also, for them, their devotion atones constantly for the murderous fantasies about him (the representative of their real father), fantasies that hark back to their infancy. Moreover, and what is even more important to the Fascist rank-and-filer, the nature of fascism is such that it provides continuously for direct expression-in-act of violence based on hatred. The hostility and aggressiveness that form the mental climate of the psychopathic are given license without end, so the lust for violence that is a condition of life for such persons is gratified as it could be under no other imaginable set of social circumstances.

If the foregoing clinical findings and sociopsychological speculations contain the measure of validity I believe they do, we find ourselves in a position now to formulate a generalization relevant to the tone and temper of these times. This generalization is not only to the effect that the political creeds that are contending so violently today reflect the character-structures of their devotees. We can go beyond this and voice a profound, scientifically derived conviction that psychopathy—psychopathy understood in its fullest psychopathological sense—is the essence of *both* of these contentious political forms.

The discovery that a particular psychological disorder lies at the core of each of the current political alternatives to democracy has immense significance.

It is a psychologically unimpeachable fact that all of us possess a measure—in some larger, in some smaller —of psychopathic potential. In each of us there lurks an infantile, asocial creature whose dormance is a necessary condition for civilized, communal life. Perhaps there will come a day when this resident antagonist will have been bred out of us, when he will no longer occupy even a corner of any of us. Certainly it is within our power to starve him out: a few generations of the kind of society that will implement rather than oppose the evolutionary tide, and the psychic parasite must perish. But meanwhile, it has to become our business to erect defenses against the recognizably psychopathic wherever they show themselves and, above all, to wage an unrelenting war against the conditions that produce them. It has already been noted that the social psychopath, the essential criminal of our time, is a world menace, a carrier of the germ of social destruction. Because he is vocal, shrewd and forceful, because he so well embodies the collective dissatisfaction which our existing society creates in the mass, he is to be feared. It is finally he who arouses the latent psychopathy in the rest of us. It is finally he who irritates our discontents and the sore spots in our personalities. It is finally he who offers us a way of "adjustment" through acting out our aggressions on the world stage—and then from our skins makes lamp shades to shield his eyes while he reads the history of a brutalized earth.

Psychopathy is a social disorder, a strange fruit

of a society's failure, beside which all the touted ills of man are about as harmless as prickly heat. While the individual instance can often be treated by deep-dynamic psychotherapy, the over-all cure rests with the cure of our society, of our social and economic system that, ignoring the psychological nature of man and insisting upon his conformity, forms a medium of frustration, insecurity and hate in which the virus of destruction breeds.

The Instinct of Rebellion

Except for those occasions when a new and startling discovery is announced, or when a controversy on some immediate public issue arises, science presents a bland surface to the world outside. The storms that rage beneath are known only to initiates, and the sometimes very hot debates that give rise to intense partisanships rarely disturb the apparent calm of the front the world perceives.

It is hardly known outside the fields involved that the question of instinct has become one of those issues about which lively argument has centered. I wish, therefore, in these pages, to defend the concept as a valid and, indeed, indispensable principle of psychology. It is also my intention to introduce certain propositions which appear to substantiate the idea that rebellion is a fundamental attribute of mankind deserving the designation of instinct.

That we should have to devote time and effort to defend the concept of instinct at all is symptomatic of current confusions. Until recently it would not have been found necessary to raise the issue, for if there was one area of agreement among us—psychologists, psychiatrists, educators, parents and all others concerned with mind and behavior—it was here; in the mutual acceptance of the proposition that instinct is an irreducible and polar consideration of the sciences and arts we practice. Today, in many quarters, the situation is different; and even where, as in psychoanalysis, the concept seems essential to the whole structure of theory and practice, doubt, hesitancy and disagreement rupture accord and interfere with progress.

I believe there are at least four reasons why it has become unfashionable—if not, in some places, actually heretical—to speak of instinct directly and without the equivocal hesitancies of certain academic psychologists, so-called neo-Freudians and others. The first and, as it will appear, the most important of these reasons, relates to the continuous if unconscious attempt of psychologists to deny the animal nature of man; the second, to the modern effort to remove psychology from the biological to the social sciences; the third, to the persistent confusion of instinct with morality; and the fourth, to an endeavor to avoid facing and solving certain disturbing matters which arise when instinct is admitted to the family of fundamental psychological concepts. It will be worth our while to attend briefly to these reasons, since they describe the sources of current perplexities so well.

The first consequence of allegiance to the proposition that human beings are, to any extent, creatures of instinct, is the immediate recognition that man is an animal. While this is an idea to which we pay lip service, it is all the same an idea we and our institutions resist. As a matter of fact, it takes very little knowledge of the world, or experience with its human-created manifestations, to perceive that it is precisely against this knowledge—and in a titanic endeavor to circumvent it—that the most elaborate defenses of mankind have been erected. Every religion, certainly, and most philosophies, have tried to deny the animal nature of man by techniques too familiar to repeat here; while custom, language, education—indeed, every other agency of human expression—have assisted them in propagating the deception. Until the Nineteenth Century of our era great success attended this effort; but in the post-Darwinian age it has become increasingly difficult to maintain the fiction. Nevertheless, it is only a mind less disciplined by the formal institutions of society, and free to accept the implications and consequences of such an idea, that can comprehend without fear the absolute animalism of the human being. Despite themselves, not too many of the psychological fraternity fall within this group. Most are too much the product of intensive efforts made to deny the fundamental nature of human nature by institutions in which they have been reared. In their thinking, then, and in their work, they reveal a kind of intellectual schizophrenia that not all of their verbal gyrations can hide from the discerning eye. For example, because instinct cements the tie that binds animal to man, they invent such totally meaningless circumlocutions as "intrinsic needs," "man's nature," "genital lust dynamisms," "energy transformations," "specific motivational potentials," et cetera. Or, while freely acknowledging a phenomenon among other species to be due to instinct, when the same phenomenon is observed among men, it is attributed, instead, to "learning," to "imitation," or to whatever defense against the instinct concept happens to be in vogue. One psychologist who has had a tremendous influence on the thinking of many of us has even gone so far as to equate the greater development of the brain as in man with a less complete and fixed instinctual equipment. Fromm and his group believe that the ability to learn more or less supplants instinct. Their formula seems to be: the more developed the brain the greater the ability to learn and the less dependence there must be on instinct. This makes an impressive and resonant noise, but it is startling in its naïveté and abysmal in its obvious ignorance of the facts of neurophysiology, biochemistry, biology and psychology, as modern research reveals them.

I have stated that the second reason why the instinct concept has been shelved has to do with the effort being exerted nowadays to displace psychology from the biological to the social sciences. This is a movement that has been going on for approximately fifty years, having its roots in the disavowal of man's animal nature and deriving from the observation that the operations and functions of men are carried out

in a social milieu. The psychologies and psychothera-
peutics stemming from this observation have uniformly emphasized those aspects of behavior which
emerge from the interactions among men, on the one
hand, and the relationships of individuals as organisms to the larger organism of society. They adopt a
viewpoint of the human that, in all essentials, de-
prives him of significance in any terms but those pre-
eminently social. His biological nature, then, becomes
lost—rather, to be more accurate, it is rendered secondary in importance to his social nature. The Field
Theory of Lewin, the Sociometry of Moreno, and the
Interpersonal Relations psychology of Sullivan all
illustrate, in their formulations, the primary position
occupied by society as the theatre of behavior and the
mutual interactionism of individuals. With all of them
man, as such, has little importance, and his characteristics as well as his functions originate from the human setting and the processes of interhuman exchange. These psychologies and their offspring—the
sociologies represented, for example, by Reisman, and
the psychotherapies of the Washington and other
schools—have not yet committed the Marxian error
of attributing fundamental human psychic phenomena to the relations, productive or otherwise, of men;
but they come uncomfortably close to that position.
What they show in common, however, is a contempt
for biology and a conscientious, if perceptibly strain-
ful, endeavor to exclude it from their theoretical, descriptive and prescriptive preoccupations. But biology

will not be excluded, nor will psychology—which remains a biological science—yield. The speculations and researches of men like E. W. Sinnott, L. J. Henderson, Joseph Needham, E. S. Russell and Herbert Muller, as well as Erwin Schrödinger, Julian Huxley and Hans Driesch—to say nothing of the psychologists themselves—are each day regaining ground that has been lost to the anti-biological forces, and are recovering psychology for the sciences that belong to the biological group.

A third reason for the rejection of instinct is, as I have stated, the confusion that exists in the modern mind between instinct and morality. This is a consequence, it would seem, of a persistent misunderstanding of what instinct is and reverts, once again, to the stubborn disavowal of their animal nature that characterizes most men, even though they be scientists or philosophers. Instinct, unhappily, has always been identified, and in some cases made synonymous, with the basic predispositions against which the defenses of society have been organized. The seven deadly sins proscribed by Judeo-Christian culture have been attributed typically to its machinations, while the virtues, such as they may be, have been ascribed either to the interference of supernatural agencies or to a divine and unhuman characteristic of man that is essentially alien to him, being given or loaned by powers beyond his ken. What is base in man is due to his instinct; what is noble to his gods. That instinct, however, is beyond good and evil, that it may account for the positive (in moral and ethical terms) as well as the negative qualities exhibited by humanoids, is hardly ever recognized. And even in quarters where this is acknowledged—among the philosophers and humanitarians—it receives but a grudging assent. Yet it remains a fact that the confusion in thought of instinct and morality, which have nothing whatever to do with each other, continues and is to be found in the works of psychologists where it exists as a tacit assumption. So, to range themselves and their ideas foursquare with regnant morality, they reject instinct, while tenets that seem to offer a way out of the apparent dilemma that instinct poses find a ready audience among them. What is wanted, of course, is more knowledge and precise definition—which would lead, if nowhere else, to a clear comprehension that instinct is *given* and *there,* outside the shifting standards, codes and conventions that reflect the culture and its institutions.

A final reason for the unpopularity of the instinct concept, and the one that applies specifically to members of the psychological fraternity, is the necessity its adoption places them under to raise and solve the problems they have inherited. Foremost among these are questions involving the "Death Instinct," the universality of the "Oedipus Complex," and its role as the parent of neuroses. These are complicated and disturbing matters, which have become issues of such importance that schisms and ruptures regularly attend their debate. We seek to avoid coming to grips with these questions. Many of us, thus motivated, have discovered that the surest way to intellectual equanimity lies in eliminating them entirely. To do this, it is of course necessary to declare against the concept of instinct from which these perplexing issues originate in the first place.

Now that we have accounted, at least in part, for the rejection of instinct that is so notorious among workers in the sciences and arts of psychology, it is pertinent to ask what instinct is. I raise this question not because any of us requires instruction, but because I believe re-definition is necessitated by the new light that has been shed on the matter from sources outside, yet allied to, our field of inquiry. I believe also that these novel formulations of the problem remove it to an entirely different frame of reference and, by doing so, undercut resistance to the concept as a whole while, at the same time, they answer many of the more valid objections raised against the employment of instinct as an irreducible and polar principle of psychology. Finally, re-definition is required here because only in the referential frame that emerges therefrom can the instinct of rebellion be comprehended.

Numerous definitions of instinct have been given us by philosophers, biologists and psychologists over the years during which the propositions basic to the sciences of life were being formulated. It remained for Sigmund Freud, however, to present the first meaningful account of the idea for psychology.*

According to the original views of Freud, instinct is a borderline concept between the mental and the organic spheres. It originates within the organism as energy directed toward an inherently determined goal and constitutes an internal stimulus to the mind. As the founder of psychoanalysis stated in his classical paper, "Instincts and Their Vicissitudes," instinct is "a measure of the demand for work imposed upon the mind in consequence of its connection with the body."

Now, as stimulus, the energy that is instinct opposes the regulative functions of the mind and creates therein a condition of tension. It is this tension that imposes upon the mental apparatus continuous demands for work, characterized by Freud as the abolition of those stimuli which reached it, the reduction

* Throughout this section I have made liberal and often direct use of many sources, including: S. Freud, Instincts and Their Vicissitudes, *Collected Papers,* IV, 1915, and *An Outline of Psychoanalysis,* Norton, New York, 1949; E. Bibring, The Development and Problems of the Theory of the Instincts, *International Journal of Psychoanalysis,* XXII, Part 2, 1941; L. Kubie, Some Implications for Psychoanalysis of Modern Concepts of the Organization of the Brain, *Psychoanalytic Quarterly,* 22, 1953; H. Hartmann, Comments on the Psychoanalytic Theory of Instinctual Drives, *Psychoanalytic Quarterly,* 17, 1948; J. Z. Young, *Doubt and Certainty in Science,* Oxford, 1951; E. W. Sinnott, *Cell and Psyche,* University of North Carolina, 1950; N. Weiner, *Cybernetics,* Wiley, 1948; W. S. McCulloch and J. Pfeiffer, Of Digital Computers Called Brains, *Scientific Monthly,* 60, No. 6, 1949; etc.

of excitation to the lowest level possible, or the maintenance of a condition of non-stimulation. Thus a
fundamental opposition was set up between mind and
instinct, an opposition arising from the nature of each
—instinct as stimulus and mind as regulative mechanism preoccupied with the reduction or elimination
of tension aroused by interior stimulation.

As to the sources of instincts, Freud specifically
placed them in the organic field, and on the basis of
this criterion was able to construct a classification of
the instincts. In his view, an organic event of a biochemical nature took place at the site of an organ.
This created the necessity for work within the mental
apparatus and led to the satisfaction (reduction or
elimination of tension) of the instinct. Since the site
of the event and the site of satisfaction ordinarily
coincided—except in the case of the component instincts—the function of that organ which contained
both origin and terminus of the organic crisis determined, for purposes of classification, the nature of the
instinct involved. So if, by a complex of biochemical
events, a tension arose in the genitalia, the mental
apparatus was employed to seek its relief by activat-
ing the area concerned. Discharge of tension through
the specific organs of sex completed the simple cycle
of the sexual instinct.

In the course of development of instinct theory,
Freud altered and modified the original schema I
have sketched. As his concepts clarified and his view,
especially of mental topography, changed, he found

it imperative to abandon the derivative and second-ary aspects of his over-all description and classification of instinct. When it became apparent to him that the ego also had fundamental characteristics which produced psychic energy, manifesting tension within the mind and stimulating it toward work of a similar nature; when he realized the sources of excitation were here diffuse and not confined to an organ or even a group of organs; and when he further discovered that in the case of the ego the organic event defied specific localization—he relinquished *source* as his criterion for classification and substituted *aim*. But this substitution in no wise radically altered his basic conception of instinct. It remained psychic energy arising from a source, directed upon an object, seeking the fulfillment of an aim. It remained also an interior stimulus for work within the mind. And it remained, furthermore, the product of an organic event. Nevertheless, aim was found more suitable for classificatory purposes, and with this the theatre of operations for instinct became enlarged; for aim consisted in the exertion of a purposive activity upon the object, which produced external results, while inwardly there occurred the attainment of aim in the relaxation of tension.

Freud was not content to allow his concept of instinct to remain fixed, and when he came to formulate the final expression of his theory of the primal instincts (the life and death instincts) he changed it completely. In his final expression, he renounced his former view of instinct as "tension of energy" demanding mental work, organically rooted, and aimed at satisfaction in the organ or sphere of origination. Now it became the directive and guiding force of the vital processes; and because he was quick to apprehend the resemblance between the mental or psychological processes and the instinctual when placed in this new perspective, he was able to achieve an absolute synthesis of instinct with the fundamental principles of life itself.

Since Freud, many theoreticians of psychoanalysis have concerned themselves with the concept of instinct. Apart from the fact that some found it impossible to follow him beyond the stage of the first qualification he made in the development of his views, there has been widespread dissatisfaction especially with the terms in which he phrased them. Need has been expressed for greater clarification of such matters as "tension," "psychic energy," "organic event," et cetera. To meet this need, it has been found necessary to call upon specialists from outside the field of psychology as such. As a result of their efforts, it would appear that we are now in a position to retain the concept of instinct—indeed, that we must adhere to it even more closely as a pillar of human psychology—but in a form that meets the modern demand for greater scientific accuracy. Parenthetically, it should be remarked here that the insights provided from allied fields substantiate, in all essentials, the

Freudian concept, at the same time as they lend it precision.

Among the fructifying contributions to a modern theory of instinct there have to be noted especially the influence of latter-day neurophysiology, biophysics, and biochemistry. As a broad definition resulting from observations and researches in these fields, perhaps G. E. Coghill's is representative. According to it, instinct is the total pattern in action. For him and others, normal growth and behavior are carried on by virtue of the dominance and regulatory control of instinct, as an integrating agency, over all local and subordinate activities of the organism, biological and psychological. The Coghillian equation, however, has been underwritten and refined. Biochemists have been able to describe the states of body fluids and tissues, both at rest and in action, and this description constitutes an enormous advance over previous methods of apprehending instinct and its operational modes. It has been established beyond equivocation that all tissues and fluids which compose the organisms maintain themselves by "flux." This produces manifold asynchronous processes, all on-going at any given moment in the history of the body, and characterize its vitality as well as its viability—even during periods of so-called rest. However, a synchronization of the myriad processes takes place under the influence (on the intake side) of deprivation, or (on the output side) under the influence of chemical accumu-

lation and physical distention. With the synchronization or mobilization into an extensive organic pattern of the separate biochemical and biophysical
processes occurring in the individual cells comprising
both tissues and fluids, a state of physiological necessity is produced over the body-as-a-whole. This syn-
chronized tissue-necessity is then represented by a
psychological state of need, craving or appetite. In
turn, such a state achieves expression by way of an
organized pattern of behavior recognized as instinctual behavior which, in effect, de-mobilizes the organic processes and returns them to their former state
of asynchronous and relatively independent operation.

The Cyberneticists, moreover, have been able to
go beyond even this rather exquisite refinement of
the concept of instinct. Led by such brilliant thinkers
as Norbert Weiner and Warren S. McCullough, and
totally unhampered by preconceptions in their remarkable efforts to formulate a science of control and
communication in the animal and the machine, they
have said what for the present seems to be the last
word on instinct. To them, we owe the definition of
instinct as *built-in possibility or potentiality* in the
organism with the express function of transmitting
information to the co-ordinating and executive cen-
tres of the brain. The information transmitted originates from biochemic and biophysic states already
described. Within the brain, which may be viewed as
an inconceivably complex computer, it initiates ac-

tivities roughly of the order of sorting and solving, and finally executes solutions along efferent pathways already existing or opened by the secondary functions such as learning.

The Cybernetic conception of the brain as a digital computer must be taken, as it is meant, in purely comparative and relative terms. Actually, as McCullough has pointed out, "A computer with as many vacuum tubes as a man has neurons in his head would require the Pentagon to house it, Niagara's power to run it, and Niagara's waters to cool it. The largest existing calculating machine has more relays than an ant but fewer than a flat worm." Nevertheless, the conception leads us to the clearest exposition of what instinct is and how it works. J. Z. Young, in his 1950 B.B.C. Reith Lectures wherein he speaks of the brain as the receptive and directive organ for the receipt and disposal of information that establishes communication within the body and between bodies, has described its essential operation and functions in remarkably simple terms. The brain system, he states, works with a very large number of units; each carries information of only a simple type; mixing places exist within it where the single channels converge; and there is feedback from every stage to the one before. The notion of feedback, of course, delineates the mechanism by which instinctual tension is allayed. H. Kalmus, elaborating on the whole cybernetical concept of instinct, takes the final step toward proposing answers to the remaining problem which in-

stinct has traditionally raised. He suggests that we
consider the genes as carriers of information from one
generation to the next. This, he believes, not only
solves the question of the presence within the organism of potentialities and possibilities, but permits
mobilization of "the whole apparatus of mathematics
that describes the transmission of information for
analyzing how the workings of the body for every moment of its life are controlled by the information it has
received from the millions of generations in the past."

So we appear to have emerged with a new concept of instinct which, in every essential, reverts to
the Freudian formulation. By taking over from allied
fields, we have achieved more precise definition, great
insight into mechanism, and enormous clarification of
terms. It is from this perspective that we are prepared, at last, to consider the validity of an instinct
I have chosen to call the "instinct of rebellion."

By the term rebellion we are to understand the
quality, common among all men and characteristic of
the species, to change the environments and circumstances comprising the medium of both individual
and social life. In contrast with other animals, man
adapts "alloplastically." The changes he effects, that
is, are wrought *by* him, rather than imposed *upon*
him.* By this trait alone does he distinguish himself

* It is to be understood here that man's capacity to adapt
alloplastically is, while rooted in instinct, implemented by
awareness and hence largely conscious in application. Certain

from all other orders of life that now inhabit the earth. By this predisposition is his human-ness established. As a dimension of man, rebellion actually defines him.

In terms of the definition we have arrived at, rebellion must be classified as an instinct. It is built into man as a possibility mediated by all the organs and tissues of the body which, singly and together, exhibit eternal restlessness, change and flux. Particularly is this true of the brain, and especially of the neopallium, that latest product of evolution which, as I believe, contains the seat of the rebellious urge. Moreover, rebellion identifies itself with the life instincts in the great dichotomy depicted by Freud, since it functions continuously in the service and affirmation of life, assisting the organism to evade decay, dissolution and death. Finally, it is suggested that rebellion, as an instinct that participates in all the activities of the organism, is the vehicle of evolution, now resident only in man and eventually to become the property of man's successor in the evolutionary chain.

These rather sweeping generalizations can be supported, I think, by an unprejudiced view of the

---

other animals, predominantly those within the direct line of human descent, or in collateral lines, also effect changes in their environs—as, for example, the beaver when he fells a tree to make his dam. But such alloplastic adaptations seem to be direct responses to immediate environmental stimuli, are entirely unconscious, temporary, discontinuous, static, and specific. Moreover, they apply only to a strictly limited number of acts; whereas in man they characterize the entire range of his behavior.

facts, as well as from the standpoint of some philosophical propositions of a relatively simple order. Elsewhere * I have described a so-called "triad of limitations," intending by this phrase to convey the notion of a hypothetical triangular enclosure in which the human specie and all other living species are imprisoned. One side of the triangle is composed of the medium provided by nature, another by their endowed equipment, and the third by the mortality of living things. Rejecting all definite teleological speculation, I have, nevertheless, identified the purpose of life with the purpose of evolution, and both with the overcoming of the limiting, enclosing triangle. To break through this prison, to escape from it, is, I believe, the purpose of life and the design of evolution.

Now, it is a hardly debatable fact that only man, among all animals, has refused to remain enclosed within the limiting triangle. While his protest against the triad of limitations was foreshadowed among forms that marked the stages of his evolution, no other kind of life sought so arduously to overcome, to master, any of the arms of the fateful triangle. "Autoplastically" oriented, other species adapted completely and so worked themselves into an evolutionary cul-de-sac, or by adaptation brought about their own elimination. Man alone, rejecting resignation, has assaulted his prison.† He has conquered his me-

* R. Lindner, *Prescription for Rebellion,* Rinehart, New York, 1952.
† Critics of my views have objected to the statement that

dium even to the extent of overcoming gravity, he has extended his endowed equipment to marvelous lengths, and he struggles relentlessly against mortality.

It would be foolish to deny that the only animal which persistently wages war against all that limits it possesses something which other forms of life lack.

---

man alone "assaults his prison." They claim that all animals which survive do so by adapting to new or unfamiliar environments, that the processes of adaptation are in themselves evolutionary and that rebellion is therefore only another and more elaborate name for a procedure long ago identified. In evidence, they characteristically offer the bacteria and viruses that show resistance to anti-biotics, and the infamous flies that seem to mock preparations like D.D.T.

Apart from the fact that this kind of criticism betrays ignorance about evolutionary theory—for adaptation through mutation is not the mechanism of evolution as it is now understood—it indicates a failure to distinguish between the types of adaptation available to organisms and a lack of appreciation for how man conducts his affairs. Most animals that survive make autoplastic adaptations: they meet presenting problems and frustrations by changing themselves. A limited number of animals, as I have already stated, effect changes in their environments—for example, there is a certain insect which ejects a fluid to neutralize the acidity of a special medium it encounters in its travels. But except for man, all other forms achieve static adaptations, be they by means of auto- or alloplasticity. That is to say, they stop at the point where the problem of frustration has been met. Their protest, even where expressed alloplastically, is not continuous. The fly does not, like man, invent a procedure to insure himself and his kind against the ravages of D.D.T., but only against the strength of a particular solution. A fur-bearing animal thickens his coat against winter, but does not provide his shelter with heat nor continue schemes that range from digging coal to storing solar energy. The problem-solving of other forms is specifically adaptive, hence static. Rebellion is dynamic.

This something must be inevitable, innate, unlearned, specialized for its cosmic tasks and yet a characteristic of the whole organism. This something, in short, must be instinct.

The manner in which this instinct expresses itself gives it its name. Because the modes of expression are typically those of protest aimed at overcoming, of discontent aimed at the elimination of the sources provoking discontent, of insurrection opposing resignation, of restlessness against passivity, and mastery against acceptance, *rebellion*, despite certain semantic objections, seems most apt as a designation.

Perhaps the largest claim made for the instinct of rebellion is that it is the vehicle of evolution. Although the claim is extensive, I find it hard to avoid. Certainly, animals which lack the instinct are static, while those which possess it, even in rudimentary form, tend to show evolutionary progress—defined, I repeat, by mastery over the triad of limitations. So the instinct emerges as the channel for fulfillment of all the possibilities of the human species and the driving force, it would seem, behind the unfolding of those processes we term, generically, as evolution. Moreover, it is at this point that a matter of great interest to thinkers and workers in the biological sciences and arts arises. If it is true that an equation exists between the instinct of rebellion and evolution, then the seat, centre, or site of the instinct within the body is not hard to find. It must be in the cerebral cortex, that part of the brain developed from the area between the pyriform lobe and the hippocampus, comprising the nonolfactory region of the pallium and attaining its maximum development in man as the greater part of the cerebral hemispheres. This cerebral cortex, evolving from the smell-brain of precedent forms, is the single significant structure that has been added to the brain. Animals in the line of man possessed its rudiments, of which vestiges remain among certain existing species. But man alone actually can show a developed cortex. What is more, some biologists, basing their conclusions on comparative studies made available from paleontology, believe there is good evidence to support the view that the neopallium is continuing to evolve. Finally, it is a generally accepted notion that consciousness also resides in the cerebral cortex, existing as dim awareness, perhaps, in precedent forms with a primitive cortex, but as increased awareness of self and world in man.° Since the direction of evolution must be toward increasing consciousness and awareness, the phenomenon of consciousness appears linked to the instinct of rebellion. Thus rebellion, the instinct that underwrites evolution, can, perhaps, be localized within the cerebral cortex. Parenthetically, this should at least give pause to those who assault that area of the brain with shock or surgery.

° The term consciousness as used here does not refer to the distinction between wakefulness and sleep, or coma and the non-comatose state. It is employed to denote a whole range of psychic phenomena, especially self-awareness and identity.

As an instinct, the urge to master and the drive to overcome enters into the total behavior of humanoids, exhibiting itself in all human activities, individual and social. It signalizes its operational presence by resistance to stasis on both of these levels, as well as by vigorous efforts that always oppose passivity wherever encountered. These "vigorous efforts" are performed by the organism as a holistic unit, by its component parts, structures and functions, and, in the social sphere, by group techniques representing an instinct common to the united individuals. In this sense, the instinct is antagonistic to adjustment and conformity, both of which must now appear as antibiological and so opposed to the very nature of the human animal. Moreover, together with other instincts, the one we are delineating has its own pathology. Since our knowledge of it is so new, however, this pathology can be described only in the broadest terms and solely by reference to the polar qualities of positive and negative. It is hypothesized that *positive* rebellion describes behavior (personal and social) that operates in the service of evolution in the sense of expressions directed toward the overcoming of the triad of limitations; while *negative* rebellion describes behavior (personal and social) that operates against evolution in the sense of expressions directed upon the maintenance of that triangle. Against this scale, the strength of the instinct can be measured and its perversions and aberrations described. On the individual level, then, the mental-motor continuum from criminosis through neurosis to psychosis indicates negative rebellion; while, on the social level, negative rebellion is revealed by the entire corpus of sociopathological manifestations culminating in war.

With the foregoing in mind, it now becomes possible to say a final word about the obligation this knowledge of the existence of an instinct of rebellion, its source, possible location, purpose and pathology, imposes on us as members of the psychological fraternity and intelligently concerned laymen. Clearly, it implies certain duties and responsibilities we cannot afford to neglect. The first among these is to explore the possibilities opened to us by this new knowledge, and the second is to seek methods and techniques by which it can be employed. Obviously, it is our task to implement positive rebellion and to discourage negative rebellion. This calls for a reexamination not only of our scientific and professional conceptions, but also our attitudes both social and specialized by the nature of our work. From this reevaluation, I believe, will emerge a new orientation of the psychological sciences, a new body of theory, and a new method of practice. Founded upon the immutable rebellious, protestant, life-affirming nature of man, it must lead to the realization of his most cherished ambitions, to the achievement of his highest goals, and to the fulfillment of his destiny as carrier and transmitter of evolution.

Must You Conform?

I.

IF ANYTHING CAN BE SAID TO CHARACTERIZE THE
TIME WE ARE LIVING IN, IT IS THE EXTREME TENSION
that exists between the individual and his society.
The pitch to which this tension has risen is something
new in history. Previously, even during periods of
social unrest, revolt, or war, there seems to have
been only occasional—and then usually local—strain
between the person and the social structure as such.
Historically, most individuals lived and died in comparative harmony with the culture to which destiny
had assigned them. That they do so no longer, that a
severe and increasing stress now marks the relationship between almost all humans and their social order, and that discord has replaced concord at every
level of the social enterprise, is due, I think, to a profound change that has been taking place in the social
rather than the individual character.

In the state we are obliged to call primitive, before the patterns of interhuman exchange resolved
into forms our historians refer to as civilizations, so-

ciety was the servant of the individuals who com-
prised it. Their creature, so to speak, it operated *for*
humans, servicing their needs and supplying them
with benefits which each in his solitude and because
of his limitations could not obtain otherwise. It protected man from his enemies, provided him with necessities, and satisfied his instinctual hunger for fel-
lowship. In return, little was asked of him beyond the
rendering of similar favors. To the extent that he required, exactly to that extent was he required to give:
his strength against the enemy, the product of his
labor, and the comfort of his presence. And while this
condition was, perhaps, far from idyllic in its internal mechanics, at the very least it formed a con-
genial medium for satisfying the basic aspirations of
both the individual and the group. The secret of this
congeniality was, of course, *consent*, which few men
could withhold since individual and social aims coincided. Society, then, could be regarded largely as
the product of its separate units, as a consensus established and maintained by its component parts, as
man himself.

This is no longer true. No more is society the
servant of man, no more does it reflect and implement
his personal requirements, no more does it find its
source in the consent of its parts, and no more can it
be held that society *is* man. For it has come about
over the centuries that the organism originally created by the participation of its individual units has
assumed a life of its own. It has also acquired a dis-

position unfriendly to humans. In short, society has become a stranger to man, and a hostile stranger at that.

Whole volumes could be devoted to a description of the processes by which the transformation I have recorded has been accomplished. An entire library of causes exists for reasons which led to the endowment of an abstraction with what amounts to independent life. Let us be content here, however, to consider what are very likely the fundamental factors in both the change of character and in the evolution of the Frankenstein monster we mean when we speak of society today.

Undeniably, one determinant of change has been the vast increase, both numerical and geographic, of the social enterprise. That which we now regard as society literally covers the entire earth and embraces such a quantity of persons that the more pessimistic of our prophets have already begun to brood on the possibility of planetary exhaustion. Formerly, it was quite otherwise. The world before the Age of Discovery not only contained fewer individuals, but much of it consisted of isolated cultures fixed at various levels of development. These social islands were excluded from the concept of his society as each person conceived it because his contact with them was minimal—assuming, in the first place, that he even knew of their existence. This is not true of the modern world, wherein hardly any such isolated cultures remain, and wherein even those that do, share the characteristics of all. Today, a single great civilization has replaced many smaller ones.

The effect of the gigantic growth of society and its resolution into an all-encompassing unit has been to create a psychic distance between it and every individual. Without special training the mind is unable to grasp a concept at once so immense and so complex. It therefore tends to distinguish what the concept embodies from itself, and by this mental maneuver, which psychologists call *projection*, endows it with a separate existence. This is essentially an act of creation, which in this case breathes life into an idea and then splits it off from the individual who birthed it by a process of mind comparable to cellular division.

A second determinant of the change in character undergone by society—also a determinant of its assumption of a life of its own—involves the disparity in aims between it and the individuals of whom it is made. In what may loosely be called its original state, since one *was* actually the other, social and personal goals were the same. The aspirations of every single man corresponded with the aspirations of most other men, and these few simple goals comprehended the total aims of the community. However, when society reached that stage of development at which social stratification appeared and classes began to evolve, consonance of aims was destroyed, and man pursued one set of dreams while his society chased another.

The history of this division between men and their culture as regards aspirations is long and interesting, but hardly relevant to this discussion. It is enough for us to note that the effect of stratification into classes was to fragment the social structure. The unity that had prevailed disappeared. As observed, it had been founded originally on consent arising from the coherence of social and personal aims. But when it was no longer possible for the whole of the culture to subscribe to a single set of aims, when goals became a function of class and each class formulated its own goals according to its own necessity, consent was withdrawn. Moreover, in the struggle of each class to obtain the services of society, and by so doing impose its aims on the entire social body, society acquired further independent characteristics. Because it could only implement the aspirations of one class, it could no longer be identified with the whole of mankind, no longer incorporated within the mental image of all men. It had to be dealt with, thereafter, as a *force*, and, according to the universal, ancient habit of humans, endowed with symbolic life—as are the elements, the passions, and the mysteries of the universe.

Competition among classes for the service of society, which by now in the minds of men had assumed the viability and the shape of some huge organism extraneous to them, further altered its character. From a willing servant of humanity, it underwent a profound and radical transformation to become its master. The story of this metamorphosis is briefly told. It reveals the final dynamic in the complex of the tension now obtaining between the individual and Society—from this point forward written with a capital S.

Since the time when class stratification destroyed the cohesiveness of the social structure, Society has belonged to whichever class ruled. Depending upon the moment of history, it has given, loaned or sold its might to the ascendant order, to the segment of the culture that achieved dominance. In so doing, in becoming the instrument through which the aspirations of the particular class were realized, Society emerged the enemy of the rest of the people, their enemy and their master.

In the foregoing I have written a deliberately anthropomorphic account of the history of man's relations with Society. I believe this to be justified by the psychological facts. Men *think* of Society along the lines I have sketched, and for the reasons I have reviewed. Moreover, not only do they endow it with human attributes, but they react toward it as if it were, indeed, a supra-human individual. This is clear from the attitudes they express toward Society, from the words they employ in discussing it, and from their actions in dealing with it.

Our survey, then, has brought us to the point where we can understand man's traditionally tense relations with Society. Now it is our task to delineate the shape and dimensions of current Society; and to study, among its many effects, the increase of this tension. It is relevant, therefore, to enquire which class rules us now and what are its aims. But before this can be done, a digression is necessary to clarify the underlying transactions.

Every phase in the history of the civilization that has finally established itself on this planet has been marked by the emergence of one class, which has distinguished itself by allegiance to a special set of values superimposed on a broader base of common human values. It has always been the abiding thesis of each emergent class that its goals not only were the correct aims to which everyone should subscribe, but that solely through their realization could the universal values be achieved. In this manner morally armed, the dominant segment has always justified, to itself and to the world, whatever techniques it employed to obtain its predominantly selfish benefits; and in this manner, also, it was able to enlist Society in its efforts first to obtain, and then to maintain, its dominant status. In the time of theocracy, when priests ruled and religious aspirations formed their goals, the neat rationalization I have described vindicated every violation of their stated high aims of human happiness and salvation. In the time of capitalism, when wealth ruled and material acquisition was the social desid-

eratum, poverty and shameless exploitation were ac-
quitted by a specious Darwinism that salved conscience with semi-scientific unguents regarding the
survival of the fittest. Today, in the birth-time of the
Mass Man, when power is the motif, revolutions for
freedom are raped under the warrant of liberty. So it
has ever been, and so it is now.

And there is still another fact to be observed before the currently emergent class can be named with
a higher degree of specificity than I have just done,
or its aims described more exactly. I refer to the kind
of *behavior* the dominant segment commands toward
the fulfillment of its aspirations, the form of conduct
it calls upon Society to impose as standard in the culture. Each ruling class, that is, devises a catalogue of
behavioral indicators to signalize its authority, to witness to itself and others its prime position among the
orders of men, and to testify to the universality of its
goals. Of Society, the creation it enlists as the instrument of its strength, it requires first that it assist in
the establishment of these behavioral tokens, then
that it exercise an unceasing vigilance that they be
expressed so long as the class remains dominant. In
theocratic times the conduct dictated was such as to
exhibit religious attitudes formalized by rituals and
observances. Capitalism requisitioned, as its testa-
ment to dominance, the practice of its special ethic
and the frenzies of labor, acquisition and display. Oligarchy, in its turn, exacts conformity.

II.

Society comprehended as a supra-individual, changed in character from servant to master and identified entirely with the aspirations of a dominant social segment, furnishes the reference-frame for an explanation of the almost intolerable tension obtaining between it and the individual of today. Clearly, this pronounced strain has to originate among the factors that now characterize Society, on the one hand, and the person, on the other. It has to originate in the nature of the supra-individual as contrasted with the nature of the mundane type, in the disparity between human aims and the aims of modern Society and, finally, in the inability or unwillingness of mankind to observe the behavioral standards commanded by Society to expedite, broadcast and illustrate its goals.

In this time, which I have suggested be identified as the birth-time of Mass Man and the dawning day of the oligarch, the social enterprise, the supra-individual we call Society, has grown so huge and so terrible in its might that the mind of man is staggered before it. Not only does it, as an organism, encompass the planet, but to meet its requirements and

tend its wants, hordes of humans devote their lives
to servicing that which was once their servant. In the
factories, on the farms, in the forests, in the mines, in
the offices, shops, warehouses and arsenals, and along
the channels of communication, transportation and
exchange, an entire species now ministers to a devouring monster that can never be satisfied, to an impal-
pable immensity that cannot even be apprehended
by the senses. This creature, furthermore, commands
a strength beyond the limits of measurement. Incal-
culable armies and forces are at its disposal, and powers of creation and destruction past the limits of im-
agination are obedient to it.

Such are the shape and dimensions of Society
today, such are the lineaments of the supra-individual
each of us confronts. It is little wonder, then, that
the contrast between this colossus and his own puny
self overwhelms man, creating a psychic distance between him and it that only the magnitudes of astron-
omy can measure. Nor is it any wonder that the strain
between them has risen to an unendurable degree,
for it is this titan that has become aligned, as ever it
has, with the emerging dominant segment of our
civilization.

The class which is emergent today, and contest-
ing for authority where it has not already captured it,
is composed of a special breed of men. These are individuals who embody within their persons all the
characteristics commonest among humans, all the

traits that seem to appear when the end-stages of a civilization come into view.* Their special features partake of those aspects of human psychology and

* I believe, along with many historians including A. J. Toynbee, that "civilizations" are valid and identifiable historical units subject to certain laws regarding birth, life-course, decay, and death. Toynbee isolates twenty-one such specimens—including the present "Western Christendom," which he dates from approximately 700 A.D.; but I am inclined to set their number at a much lower figure. The criteria I employ, however, are psychological (since I am a psychologist) and not historical, and have to do with phenomena that originate in the minds of men, particularly in their unconscious. For example, I am convinced that the end-stages of any given civilization are marked by the appearance of a "new" breed of men, whose genesis may be discovered among the conditions that conspire to petrify the forms by which the given civilization or society has chosen to express itself. These men, I think, are always psychopathic, dedicated to action and violence rather than contemplation and compassion. They prepare the way for the elevation of a Leader, and on his assumption, and thereafter in his name, rule. He, in turn, carries the unconscious drama one step further by getting himself killed and immolated. By his death he brings about the blood-bath in which the civilization dissolves; while elsewhere another society is being born—to follow the same unconsciously motivated timeless cycle.

I am further convinced that the "cycle of civilizations," the eternal round of societal birth-and-death, can be broken, now that we possess a tool for understanding it in psychoanalysis. It was only man's ignorance of himself that sustained it, anyhow. The question is: will we employ this knowledge?

However, for the purposes of this essay, one certainly does not have to subscribe to the general psycho-historical theory of civilizations I have proposed here and elsewhere (especially in *Prescription for Rebellion*, Rinehart, New York, 1952). It remains a fact that an oligarchy composed of psychopathic-like men *is* emergent; and the psychologist, knowing how such men think and behave, can make a reasonable prophecy as to the future.

behavior that are uncovered when the control of
Society finally passes from human hands, when Society begins to loom so enormously (as it does currently) over men, when it oppresses them. In the
phase of history of a civilization that denies humans
access to the springs of instinctual satisfaction, that
frustrates their desires, that displaces them from ac-
customed positions in the social order, that, in sum-
mary, weakens their individual egos to the point
where independent identity is lost, the uniqueness of
the person disappears and man dissolves into the
mass. Assisted by historic and psychological processes I have labelled elsewhere—processes I have
called *urbanization, standardization,* and *proletarian-
ization* (with the latter term being understood in a
special sense)—men at first mentally, then physi-
cally, begin to herd.* Out of their herding and conceived from their despair are born the new men, who
now form a class that takes charge of the collectivity,
personates its distinguishing attributes, and domi-
nates by catering to the basest in the nature of humans.

Who are these new men, these leaders behind
whom the masses march, these shepherds of humanity who herd the millions of earth into slave labor
camps and crematoria; and what do they want, what
are their aims?

They are the prototype of mediocrity, the incar-
nation of the average. In face and form they could

* *Op. cit.,* 168ff.

be anyone; in fact they are everyone. The common-place, the vulgar and the unexceptional stamp them. Whether they be called by the names of Franco, Khrushchev, or McCarthy, they are essentially anonymous, as anonymous as Hoffer's "True Believer," Koestler's "Commissar," or "Big Brother" of the Orwellian nightmare—for they, like their charges, but to a degree more profound, are the unidentified, the frustrated, the truly inadequate, and the displaced.

The designation that best fits the demagogues who comprise our emergent dominant class, who now contend for rule over parts of the earth they do not already control, and who, I believe, are coming into their own age, is the psychiatric diagnosis of *psychopathic personality*. This describes them exactly. This is what they are and this is what they represent of the people: the psychopathy latent in all men, the madness which suffering and oppression uncover. They are the perfect expression of Mass Manhood who betray every symptom of the disorder that afflicts man at that moment of history when it is hardly possible for him to be human any longer. As such, these leaders, like illustrations in a clinical text, faithfully mirror in their lives and their actions the epidemic of psychopathy which spreads everywhere in mankind's "time of troubles." The perfection of their psychopathy is what suits them for leadership. Unlike the Mass Man whose capacity for psychopathic behavior emerges only in the medium of the collectivity and under the sanction of a master, the type of ruler of

whom we speak now is born and bred to the psychopathic estate. On the way to rule he runs through the
alphabet of acts and symptoms that typify the condition—as witness the career of Stalin; and as ruler, he
continues to manifest them, but now with a largeness
and on a scale commensurate with his position of
overlordship—as witness Hitler in the days of his tyranny.

We turn now to the question: what do these
leaders want?

The answer is simple: they want power. But the
kind and degree of power they want is one which
decent and not-yet psychopathic men find hard to
conceive of, much less to define.

There are two approaches to the problem of apprehending the meaning of power in the present as
contrasted with its meaning in the past. These approaches involve the problems of *why* and *how much*.

In the past, as now, of course, power was used to
maintain itself. Beyond this, however, it had an additional purpose, which was always to provide the
ruling class with some specific benefit, some set of defined values, some result of the application of power
which they could use, treasure, exchange or exhibit.
So, when the priests of theocratic times ruled, the
purpose of power was salvation for the rulers and
those who were ruled, the benefits granted by God
or the gods, and the temples, palaces, and other ob-
jects that certified the cultural values. So also, when

capitalists constituted the ruling class, the purpose of power was the acquisition of personal wealth and its transmission through the generations, as witnessed by the display or hoarding of money. And so it was with every dominant segment of the social order—of which these are but two examples—throughout history. In each case, it should be noted, power was used for something else.

As for the problem of how much power was employed to obtain the desired aim or to reach the sought-for goal, in bygone times this was always determined by necessity, which in turn was defined by the point at which the value or benefit was realized. To remain with our examples: during the theocracy, power was applied to the degree necessary to convert the infidel, appease the gods, save the heretic or accomplish whatever the particular situation demanded. For example, when the confession of faith was made, no matter what the techniques were that had obtained it, the pressure of power was withdrawn; or, as another instance, when the rains finally came, the sacrifice of items sacred to the rainmaking force ceased. With capitalism, despite its notorious insatiability, something similar occurred. Like all other ruling orders it applied power, whether of arms or men, only so long as and in the amount necessary to achieve its peculiar goals.

Power in the present, however, solves the problems of why and how much by eliminating them. To the "why is power employed?" it replies, "for no other

reason than the employment of it"—and, indeed,
those who apply it obtain no benefit from its use and
no result except the ever-increasing opportunity to
use power. To the "how much power is necessary?"
it replies, "all power, power without end"—and, indeed, there are no limits or constraints set upon
power in the modern world.

So we are confronted, today, by a wholly new
and incredible concept of power, a concept that must
include the dimensions of purity, nakedness, and ab-
soluteness. By it, not only is matter altered, but minds
atomized, identities destroyed, and personalities de-
humanized. In *1984*, such power is described and defined thusly: O'Brien, the inquisitor, has just asked
Winston Smith, the non-conformist, why the Party
wants power, and has received an unsatisfactory reply. O'Brien speaks:

> "Now I will tell you the answer to my
> question. It is this. The Party seeks power en-
> tirely for its own sake. We are not interested in
> the good of others; we are interested solely in
> power. Not wealth or luxury or long life or
> happiness; only power, pure power. What pure
> power means you will understand presently. We
> are different from all the oligarchies of the past
> in that we know what we are doing. All the
> others, even those who resembled ourselves,
> were cowards and hypocrites. The German
> Nazis and the Russian Communists came very
> close to us in their methods, but they never
> had the courage to recognize their own motives.

They pretended, perhaps they even believed, that they had seized power unwillingly and for a limited time, and that just round the corner there lay a paradise where human beings would be free and equal. We are not like that. We know that no one ever seizes power with the intention of relinquishing it. Power is not a means; it is an end. One does not establish a dictatorship in order to guard a revolution; one makes the revolution in order to establish the dictatorship. The object of persecution is persecution. The object of torture is torture. The object of power is power. Now do you begin to understand me?"

Then later:

"We are the priests of power," he said. "God is power. But at present power is only a word so far as you are concerned. It's time for you to gather some idea of what power means. The first thing you must realize is that power is collective. The individual has power only in so far as he ceases to be an individual. You know the Party slogan 'Freedom is Slavery.' Has it ever occurred to you that it is reversible? Slavery is freedom. Alone—free—the human being is always defeated. It must be so, because every human being is doomed to die, which is the greatest of all failures. But if he can make complete, utter submission, if he can escape from his identity, if he can merge himself in the Party so that he *is* the Party, then he is all-powerful and immortal. The second thing for you to re-

alize is that power is power over human beings.
Over the body—but, above all, over the mind.
Power over matter—external reality, as you
would call it—is not important."

And still later:

> ". . . Power is in inflicting pain and hu-
> miliation. Power is in tearing human minds to
> pieces and putting them together again in new
> shapes of your own choosing."

III.

And now . . . *must* you conform, *must* we conform? This is the question that confronts every man
today, the question that must be answered before
silence descends and the voice of humanity fades to
a whimper. It is a question only a few fortunate ones
can still ask, a question that cannot even be raised
behind the barbed wire where half of humanity lives.

Must we conform? Must we fit ourselves into
the pattern that molds Mass Man? Must we bend,
submit, adjust, give in? Must we, finally, cease to be
men?

The forces of Society tell us that we must.
Aligned already with the emergent dominant class,
they and the institutions they represent have put

individuality and liberty on the sacrificial altar. For a brief moment of respite, and in the vain hope that they will in this way themselves escape a destiny just over the horizon, they have become its heralds. In chorus, these forces proclaim the myth that smooths the way of the conqueror and robs their fellows of the will to resist tyranny.

Abroad in the world today is a monstrous false-hood, a consummate fabrication, to which all social agencies have loaned themselves and into which most men, women and children have been seduced. In previous writings, I have called this forgery "the Eleventh Commandment"; for such, indeed, has become the injunction: You Must Adjust!

Adjustment, that synonym for conformity that comes more easily to the modern tongue, is the theme of our swan song, the piper's tune to which we dance on the brink of the abyss, the siren's melody that destroys our senses and paralyzes our wills. But this is something known only to the few who have penetrated its disguises and glimpsed the death's head beneath: for the many, adjustment is the only way of life they know, the only way of life permitted to them by the powers that govern their existences from cradle to grave.

You must adjust . . . This is the motto inscribed on the walls of every nursery, and the processes that break the spirit are initiated there. In birth begins conformity. Slowly and subtly, the infant is shaped to the prevailing pattern, his needs for love and care turned against him as weapons to enforce submission. Uniqueness, individuality, difference—these are viewed with horror, even shame; at the very least, they are treated like diseases, and a regiment of specialists are available today to "cure" the child who will not or cannot conform. Does he violate the timetable of Gesell?—Call the pediatrician, quickly! Does he contradict Spock?—Get the telephone number of the nearest child analyst! Is he unhappy? maladjusted? lonely? too noisy? too quiet? too slow? too fast?—Let us be thankful for the special schools, the nurseries and, above all, for the magazines on the rack at the corner drugstore!

You must adjust . . . This is the legend imprinted in every schoolbook, the invisible message on every blackboard. Our schools have become vast factories for the manufacture of robots. We no longer send our young to them primarily to be taught and given the tools of thought, no longer primarily to be informed and acquire knowledge; but to be "socialized"—which in the current semantic means to be regimented and made to conform. The modern report card reflects with horrible precision the preoccupations of our teachers and the philosophy of our educators. Today, in the public schools, grades are given for the "ability" of a child to "adjust" to group activities, for whether he is "liked" by others, for whether he "enjoys" the subjects taught, for whether he "gets along" with his schoolmates. In the private schools, especially in those which designate themselves "progressive," the situation is more frightening, in some cases known to me actually revealing a cynical kind of anti-intellectualism. So the school takes up where the parent leaves off; and the children who emerge from it with a few shreds of individuality clinging to their blue jeans or bobby-socks are rare birds, indeed. But even if they manage to retain some uniqueness after passing through the mill of primary and secondary education, the young who go on to institutions of higher learning are exposed to pressures to conformity that must surely deprive them of the pitiful remnants of singularity and independence they still have.

In the colleges and universities it is not necessarily the teachers or the system of education that command adjustment, although currently, with academic freedom under attack and access to knowledge blocked, professors live in fear of saying or doing anything unorthodox. Here the Eleventh Commandment is more often enjoined by the young themselves upon themselves. By this time completely enslaved by the myth, they have acquired title to it, and now it comprises almost the whole of their philosophy and the basis of their code of conduct. This phenomenon, moreover, is a recent one, apparently dating from the last war. It has been brought to my attention by teachers in many colleges I have visited during the last few years. The collegian of today, they tell me, is hardly to be compared with the student of, say, twenty years ago. Today's undergraduate is almost a caricature of conformism. Like the new uniform he wears—the uniform of the junior executive that is *de rigueur* on Madison Avenue—his opinions, attitudes, tastes and behavior are ultra-conservative. In the world that is being born he will have little conflict about exchanging his charcoal grays for the deeper black of the élite guard.

You must adjust . . . This is the command etched above the door of every church, synagogue, cathedral, temple, and chapel. It constitutes a passport to salvation, an armor against sin: it sums the virtues and describes the vices. For there is no formal religion that does not insist, as its first requirement, on a confession of conformity. Nor is there, any longer, a religion that offers a path to Heaven other than the autobahn of submission. One and all, they have conspired, in the name of the Spirit, against the spirit of man: one and all, they have sold him into slavery. Under threat of damnation, hell-fire, purgatory, eternal non-being or even re-incarnation as some lower form of life, they have ordered him to renounce protest, to forego revolt, to be passive, to surrender. And while most of them were founded upon protest and by rebellion, these are the very things they now uniformly hold in horror. With Caesar and poverty, with war and hate, with disease and violence, with famine, crime and destruction, our priests, ministers, rabbis, imams, yogin, hierophants and lamas have signed a treaty to guarantee human tractability. All they have to sell us subverts the nature of man. Conformity, humility, acceptance—with these coins we are to pay our fares to paradise. Meanwhile, we must adjust, we must accept. And among the things we are to accept, in our time, are the following: riot guns, tear gas, trans-hydrogen explosives, character assassination, radioactive dust, tanks, nerve gases, guilt by association, atomic submarines, concentration camps, gas masks, guided missiles, censorship over thought and expression, rubber hoses, bacteriological warfare, purges, slave labor, bomb shelters, liquidations, brain-washing, Roy Cohn's opinions and Bishop Sheen's God . . .

You must adjust . . . This is the slogan emblazoned on the banners of all political parties, the inscription at the heart of all systems that contend for the loyalties of men. Our lives today, more than ever before, are governed by politics. Some observers, as a matter of fact, insist that modern man be called *homo politicus;* for there is hardly an area of existence that remains untouched by politics, hardly an act that in some way does not involve the manner in which our social affairs are regulated or the principles by which they are determined. Love, hate, friendship, enmity—these and other emotions have come to have political significance and, to some extent, to involve political choices. But there is no freedom even here, since conformity is of the essence of all the organizations that rule over us. Paradoxically, the systems which most loudly proclaim the right of human liberty and offer themselves as the instruments of change are those systems that oppress most heavily. On the way to power their sole condition is discipline, the severe regulation of mind and act so that the aim of the organization, the seizure somehow of power, can be achieved. At this stage of struggle, the surrender of individuality is urged or forced, but those of whom conformity is exacted are the voluntary adherents, the dedicated, the passionate few who believe truly in the slogans, in the high-sounding words of deliverance from slavery, and give over their selves to the Party. Once in power, however, what has been the dedication of a few is elevated to the religion of the many. In the congealing amber of politics the individual is pressed and imprisoned. The erstwhile revolutionary, no longer rebel but policeman and bureaucrat, becomes an oppressor; and against the revolution he has wrought he now turns—or, becoming a heretic, he dies. Meanwhile, for the masses, what has been an act of faith is now an order to surrender. Simple discipline, obedience and passivity are not enough when the Party becomes the All, for only in the collective orgasm of conformity can power be affirmed. Now is the day of the Committee, the high noon of the Inquisitor, the time of the midnight awakening, the bright lights, the spittle in the face and the breaking of bones, the long corridor, the Confession, and the merciful bullet in the back of the head.

You must adjust . . . This is the creed of the sciences that have sold themselves to the status quo, the prescription against perplexity, the placebo for anxiety. For psychiatry, psychology and the medical or social arts that depend from them have become devil's advocates and sorcerers' apprentices of conformity. Joined in the criminal conspiracy against human nature, they have poisoned the last oasis for the relief of man. Of all betrayals, their treachery has been the greatest, for in them we have placed our remaining hope, and in them, sadly, hope has fled. Equating protest with madness and non-conformity with neurosis, in the clinics and hospitals, the consulting rooms and offices, they labor with art and skill to gut the flame that burns eternally at the core of being. Recklessly and with the abandon of some demented sower of noxious seeds, they fling abroad their soporifics, their sedatives, their palliative drugs and their opiate dopes, lulling the restlessness of man, besotting him so that he sleepwalks through his days and does not recognize the doom-writing on the wall. Or with the soft persuasion and counsel that apes wisdom, with pamphlets and tracts and books that flow over the mind and drown it in a rising flood of imbecilic recipes for contented existence, they prepare his ankles for chains, his back for the brand, and his head for a crown of thorns. But if these do not "cure" him into conformity, do not level him into the mass, there remain in the arsenals of adjustment the ultimate weapons: the little black box for shock "therapy" and the swift and silent knife for psychosurgery. From the skies the lightning and the thunder are

stolen to be discharged into the brain, the seat of reason, the home of evolution and the treasury of manhood. In the convulsion that follows, resistance ebbs
and another sheep is added to the flock. Or the scalpel, quiet and sterile, probes with unerring aim toward the target behind the eyes . . . up, down, to
one side, then the other . . . and a walking zombie,
the penultimate conformist, stands where a man once
stood, "cured" of his humanity.*

IV.

The question remains: must we conform? Or
can we, somehow, resist the powers that conspire to
domesticate us? Can we woo or win our liberty from
an emergent dominant segment devoted to raw
power? Can we, in short, recover Society for all hu-

* There are certain situations wherein the use of shock
therapy or psychosurgery is justified by medical necessity, but
occasions for resorting to such "heroic" techniques grow fewer
as time and research go on. Despite this, the statistical fact
is that these drastic measures are applied with increasing frequency amounting almost to abandon. One must therefore
suspect that the black box and scalpel are often used to sustain the myth of the medicos' magic powers and to obtain
quick and cheap—even if impermanent—"cures." Undeniably,
the real if unconscious aim of many psychiatrists and physicians is to subdue the patient by such means, to force him into
line, and to stamp out his distressing and stubborn tendency
toward non-conformity.

manity? And if so, with what arms are we to redeem our almost-lost manhood? How can we withstand the total onslaught I have hardly begun to describe? Where are we to find the weapons of resistance?

I believe that the question of conformity, in the long run, answers itself. I think that if there was a possibility, once, of a yes or no—if at one time humans could decide "we must conform" or "we must not"—that possibility has been lost in the long reaches of evolution, far back along the corridors of Time. The simple truth, stark and severe in its simplicity, is that *we cannot conform;* for it seems there is an ingredient in the composition of our cells, a chemistry in our blood, and a substance in our bones that will not suffer man to submit forever.

Built into man, the foundation of his consciousness, the source of his humanity and the vehicle of his evolution up from the muck of a steaming primeval swamp, is an instinct. I have chosen to call it the "instinct of rebellion," since it reveals itself as a drive or urge toward mastery over every obstacle, natural or man-made, that stands as a barrier between man and his distant, perhaps never-to-be-achieved but always-striven-after goals. It is this instinct that underwrites his survival, this instinct from which he derives his nature: a great and powerful dynamic that makes him what he is—restless, seeking, curious, forever unsatisfied, eternally struggling and eventually victorious. Because of the instinct of rebellion man has never been content with the limits of his body:

it has led him to extend his senses almost infinitely, so that his fingers now probe space, his eyes magnify the nuclei of atoms, and his ears detect whispers from the bottoms of seas. Because of the instinct of rebellion man has never been content with the limits of his mind: it has led him to inquire its secrets of the universe, to gather and learn and manipulate the fabulous inventory of the cosmos, to seek the very mysteries of creation. Because of the instinct of rebellion, man has never been content, finally, with the limits of his life: it has caused him to deny death and to war with mortality.

Man is a rebel. He is committed by his biology *not* to conform, and herein lies the paramount reason for the awful tension he experiences today in relation to Society. Unlike other creatures of earth, man cannot submit, cannot surrender his birthright of protest, for rebellion is one of his essential dimensions. He cannot deny it and remain man. In order to live he must rebel. Only total annihilation of humanity as a species can eliminate this in-built necessity. Only with the death of the last man will the revolt that is the essence of his nature also die.

But this is cold comfort in the present when the forces of conformity have collected against the spirit of man. It offers us, in the modern world, faced as we are with these forces, little satisfaction to know that the destiny of man is to conquer and that the final victory will be his.

What about now? What about today?

I suggest that the answer to the all-important question in the here and now lies in the mobilization and implementation of the instinct of rebellion. We must, in short, become acquainted with our protestant nature and learn how to use it in our daily lives, how to express it ourselves, how to infuse it throughout all levels of our culture, and how to nourish it in our young.

Today, in the struggle between man and Society over the issue of conformity, Society is winning because man, the rebel, does not yet know how to rebel successfully—positively. His protest is expressed in negative forms, in ways which may discharge somewhat the energy of his rebellious instinct but which yield him little profit; indeed, in ways which are often actually harmful to himself and to the community. Non-conformity, as it is now conceived, is largely exhibited as psychosis, neurosis, crime, and psychosomatic illness; or it appears as pitifully hopeless and vain little defiances of convention and custom in dress, manner, opinion and taste. All of these ways are negative, unproductive, totally inadequate to meet the situation man faces.

The productive way toward non-conformity is the way of positive rebellion, of protest that at once affirms the rebellious nature of man *and* the fundamental human values. These values reside in the common treasury of humanity. They form the basic aspirations of all humans everywhere and are expressed most clearly in the great documents and contracts—such as our own Bill of Rights—which men have seen fit to declare from time to time. *Rebellion and protest in their name, and conducted in a fashion which does not in any way violate their spirit, is positive rebellion, authentic rebellion.*

Our instruction in the methods of positive rebellion, of affirmative protest, must come from two sources—one inner, one outer. The first of these, the inner source, is the slower and less dependable one. It requires that men themselves awaken to the knowledge, first, that rebellion is native in them and that there exist positive ways of protest which await discovery. The inspiration and example of the all-too-few positive rebels in our culture may assist this admittedly protracted and precarious self-awakening by contagion.

The outer source of instruction is more rapid and more sure. It consists of direct tuition in positive rebellion by those to whom we have always looked, and will always look, for edification: our psychologists, educators, and artists.

While it is true, as I have charged, that these guides in human affairs have always identified with —and in some cases sold themselves to—the emerging dominant segment; and while it is true that in the current crisis they have shamefully ranged themselves on the side of conformity, it is no less true that they have done so largely out of desperation and ignorance. They have not known about the instinct at the very navel of man's being, and in their unawareness have been forced into the position they now occupy. But if once they become informed, if once they learn about the existence of such an instinct and its cosmic possibilities, it is unavoidable that the motives which inspired them toward the vocation they practice will fuse with this knowledge and become animated by it. In this manner will the methods of positive rebellion, of life-affirming protest, be explored and spread about.

The answer to the question, "Must we conform?" is a resounding No! *No* . . . not only because, in the end, we are creatures who cannot conform and who are destined to triumph over the forces of conformity; but *no* because there is an alternate way of life available to us here and now. It is the way of positive rebellion, the path of creative protest, the road of productive revolt. This is the way natural to man, the way he must and will take to achieve the values he aspires to just because he is human. By taking it, man can find the future of which he dreams, the future in which he will achieve his far, high, and unforeseeable goals . . .

Education for Maturity

THIS IS THE DAY OF THE PSYCHOLOGICAL MOUNTEBANK. EVERYONE WITH ACCESS TO PRINT APparently conceives of himself as a psychologist, and few hesitate to pontificate about man, his nature, his mind, and his future.

One of the effects of this widespread psychologizing is a loss of precision in many of the key concepts important for the study of human behavior. Somewhere in the process of verbal mauling, words and ideas that have been arrived at laboriously in science or philosophy become vague and essentially meaningless. They acquire new semantic alliances which, in time, so distort them that they are rendered completely useless for the further pursuit of knowledge.

Such a word is *maturity*, and such a fate seems to be in store for it. Depending upon which pseudo-psychological book heads the non-fiction best-seller lists, the popular meaning of maturity changes. On one Sunday morning it seems to have something to do with the wilful denial of instincts, so that the average reader is presented with the portrait of a mature person as one who renounces all temptation by the

183

cultivation of will through noble renunciation; on the next Sunday, maturity is connected with the exploitation of what's called "productivity," as if the world were a giant classroom for occupational therapy and busy hands the key to its treasures; on the third, with the achievement through dedication of an anemic and sexless kind of love; and on the fourth, with resignation in the face of the inevitable.

Were it not that these absurd definitions of maturity are seized upon so hungrily by parents and teachers for whom the printed word over the signature of a doctor or a divine has an oracular status, one could only admire the inventive and imaginative genius of their authors. As matters stand, however, our admiration must not be permitted to conceal the fact that not only is there lacking a consensus of opinion on what maturity is, but that all popular definitions are false and misleading, being based, commonly, on a prevailing misconception.

I am of the opinion that the definitions of maturity which assail us in such profusion currently are uniformly founded on the tacit hypothesis that human development is linked to human passivity. All that I have encountered assume that adjustment and conformity are the desirable modes of life, and that the closer one comes to a condition of domestication, the more mature one is. None of them, to my knowledge, takes account of man's nature and spirit, of his innate rebelliousness, of his intrinsic values, or of his individuality. With monotonous regularity, these definitions predicate themselves upon, and defend, a society that is everyday and everywhere becoming more and more oppressive. Hence, the standards for mature behavior they advise are those standards that may apply to mature cattle or mature puppets—but not to mature men.

For a concept of maturity to have any validity it must, first of all, take the measure of man. It must proceed from a knowledge of what he is and must extend, through an appraisal of his potentialities, to a knowledge of where he is going. To know what he is involves the study of the roots and sources of his behavior; to know where he is going involves the study of his aims and values.

Science has been able to tell us much about what man is. It has defined his dimensions to a remarkable degree, and while on most scores it still lacks precision, it has reached a point where many mysteries of the psychosomatic unit have succumbed to analysis and measurement. Among these dimensions is the psychological, which consists of the instincts that determine behavior, the modes and channels that express behavior and, finally, the products and results of behavior as they appear in the individual's performance both alone and in society. Of all of these, at once the most important because it is basic and the most difficult to comprehend because it is elusive, the instinctual level describes human nature. In doing so, it establishes kinship between the human and other species; also, it draws the distinction, in fundamental terms, between the animal we call man and remaining forms of life.

The quality that sets man apart, clearly and radically proclaiming his difference, is a forward-pressing urge that has made him the instrument of evolution. It is an instinct which only he possesses to more than a vague and tentative degree, a drive which is literally built into the fibre of his being. I have characterized this instinct as one of rebellion, indicating by the use of that term a chronic state of protest leading to an unvarying potential for action aimed at mastery over the limiting conditions of existence. I will not pause here to justify the concept of rebellion as an instinct or to debate its merits, since I have covered these matters elsewhere. However, it is important to note that his rebelliousness appears to be the essence of man's nature, the theme of his life and the meaning—if there is any at all—of his existence. These extensive propositions are justified by reference to an observation concerning the conditions under which all forms exist, an observation with broad philosophical, psychological and (as we shall see) educational implications. I refer to what may be called the "triad of limitations," the triangular set of factors that comprise an existential perimeter for all being.

Life is locked within a three-sided enclosure which evolution seeks to pierce. One arm of this prison consists of the medium in which existence occurs, another of the endowed equipment with which forms are provided, and a third of the mortality to which forms succumb. It is into this cage that all animals are thrust. Most live and die therein. Some few strain against one or another of its sides. But only man assaults this citadel and attempts persistently, arduously and successfully to break through. The wall of the medium he has already surmounted, until now he stands poised on a springboard into Space. The wall of endowed equipment is crumbling before his onslaught, until now his arms encircle the planet, his eyes see through darkness, and his ears hear the murmurings of plants. As for the wall of mortality, it also gives way, perhaps more slowly, but inevitably, before his deliberate advance. These things man does because there is a necessity in him to do them, a necessity that drives him to overcome and master the limits of existence, a rebellious inclination that forces him to protest and to refuse to be bound.

We can measure both progress and value by reference to the triad of limitations and the instinctual necessity which urges the human animal, alone among the forms of life, to assail it. *Progress* emerges, then, as a scale marked off by units recording the dissolution or decomposition of the barriers that comprise the enclosing triangle; while *value* derives from the idea that, since the purpose of life is apparently to eliminate the perimeters of existence, anything which serves this purpose must be good.

With these basic propositions established, it is evident that we are approaching a definition of maturity based solidly on a knowledge of human nature, on the one hand, and the meaning of existence on the other. However, before we can achieve this definition, we have to return briefly to the instinct of rebellion and consider the question of its vicissitudes.

Like all instincts, rebellion has its versatility, its mutability, its fluctuations and its pathology. At present, I know of no other way to describe these than by reference to the polar aspects of the instinct; that is, in terms of its negative and positive expressions. Broadly speaking, negative rebellion is conduct expressive of the raw drive to protest and with little or no relation to the ends of progress and value attached to mastery of the limiting triad. It is adventitious rebellion, rebellion for its own sake, rebellion without a cause. Individuals whom we call *psychopathic personalities,* for example, illustrate negative rebellion most clearly. Positive rebellion, however, differs sharply. It consists of conduct expressive of the same drive, but aimed at the realization of both value and progress. It is protest with a meaning, rebellion with a cause. And since, as Albert Camus has recently pointed out, every act of positive rebellion tacitly invokes a value, but ceases to be positive the moment this value is betrayed, it accomplishes its end solely by virtue of means which in themselves consistently maintain the value.

From all of this, it finally emerges that *maturity means positive rebellion, and that the mature person is the positive rebel.* The absolute criterion of maturity, then, consists of the capacity to employ the instinct of rebellion in positive ways for the achievement of values arising from the nature of man, the conditions of his life, and the aspirations and purposes of his existence.

No one can question that the mature person, the positive rebel, is essential to our society. The maintenance of our values and their realization depends upon him, as does our progress. Indeed, our fate is in his hands—and not only ours specifically, but the fate of evolution. Therefore, it becomes our duty to seek ways and means of producing mature persons and of increasing their number among us. Let us, then, turn to the question of how this can be done.

Unless our geneticists someday discover the secret of breeding the positive rebellious type, he will always have to be reared and educated. From the moment of birth until he achieves maturity, the fires of his innate rebellion will have to be tended. By the conjoint efforts of his parents and teachers, the instinct that underwrites his life will require the careful nurturing due something infinitely precious, treasured and cared for, so that it will grow strong within him and be pointed firmly toward the positive pole of his existence. For them to do this, however, demands a dedication few possess, an understanding many lack, and a spirit now foreign to most who have the care, rearing and education of children in their hands.

The first requisite for a teacher or parent who

wishes to assist the evolutionary process by rearing
our young toward genuine maturity is that he root
out from himself every last vestige of the myth of adjustment. He must exorcise from his heart and mind,
and from his behavior, adulation of the fiction of conformity that has brought society within sight of
doomsday and that threatens to engulf the world in
another long night of medievalism. He must deny
that passivity, surrender, conformism and domestication pave the road to human happiness and salvation.
Instead, he must affirm the rights of protest and individuality, encourage uniqueness, and be unshaken
in an abiding faith that only in these ways will he
discover himself and the true vocation of his life.

   This is a large order, and one that few can fill. It
demands an orientation that is unfamiliar to us, and
it calls for a sharp break with the past. We—parents
and teachers—have been reared in a society dedicated to the proposition that man has to adjust to
the conditions of the world around him or be damned.
Every institution of the culture we have permitted to
be reared over us—and all of the agents of these institutions to whom we have entrusted ourselves—have
demanded the sacrifice of both individuality and freedom. They have decreed that protest is sinful, non-
conformity criminal, and uniqueness a disease. Unan-
imously, they have published an addendum to the
Decalogue: You must adjust!—And in the service of
this de-humanizing commandment they have mobi-
lized powers ranging from the disapproving look on

a mother's face to the concentration camp, from the admonishing finger of a teacher to the electric-shock box. These have bent our wills and broken our spirits, and to defy them takes extraordinary courage. Yet, if we are even to approach the task of educating for maturity, defy them we must. Only when we have thus broken with the past will we be fit to cultivate the future.

The first step toward the production of positive rebels is taken, therefore, when their parents and teachers assume a new orientation. Following this, the procedure is one that encourages the acquisition of those traits the mature person regularly demonstrates as characteristics of his personality. It is to them that we will now attend.

There are very likely more, but until now I have been able to isolate only six attributes of the positively rebellious individual—six signs by which the mature person can be distinguished. I have labelled them: *awareness; identity; skepticism; responsibility; employment;* and *tension.** Since these are common words used in an uncommon sense, and since each

* Since the publication of *Prescription for Rebellion* (Rinehart and Company, New York, 1952), I have devoted much of my time to seeking additional attributes of maturity. I have searched the literature, observed people carefully, and talked or corresponded with many of the leaders of science and thought in connection with my quest. So far, I have discovered nothing which cannot be reduced to or be included among the original six identificatory qualities. I urge the participation of my readers in this search and hopefully invite their assistance.

designates a whole realm of experience and behavior, they require both explanation and precise definition.

Awareness has to do with the enlargement of consciousness and the extension of cortical control in our lives. The kind of consciousness implied here, however, is not the state of wakefulness as contrasted with the condition of coma or sleep, but consciousness in its profounder meaning of increased capacity for the utilization of bodily equipment, of the extension of self-knowledge, of the understanding of motivation, and of independence from crippling unconscious sources of thought and act.

The problem of enlarging consciousness has intrigued men since before history was recorded. Correctly, advanced thinkers in every age have understood that the world immediately accessible to the senses was incompletely presented because of the inadequacy of those very senses; and also that by the application of their in-built capacity for storing and manipulating items of knowledge, they could obtain an enormously increased apprehension of—and therefore a control over—their environment. Their attempts to enlarge consciousness accordingly took two directions. Concentrating on the sensory approach, some veered off onto paths leading toward mysticism. By introducing foreign substances into their bodies —substances such as drugs or gases that were (and are) considered to induce a hyperacuity of the senses —they were brought to experience certain remarkable effects which, so they believed, transcended reality. Among this group, also, are numbered those who, alternatively but for the same reasons, undertook to achieve this desired enlargement of consciousness by establishing rigorous, sometimes painful discipline over their bodies through yoga-like exercises or the inhibition of instinctual cravings like those for food or sex.

The second direction the quest took led to science. Out of the chaos presented to men by the separate items of life and their direct experience of the world, order was created, relationships were observed, and methods for comprehending, then extending, man's grasp of the universe discovered. The instrument responsible for this technique of enlargement was the brain itself, and the methods comprising the technique those of that highly specialized organ, *e.g.*, reason.

A third path of enlargement of consciousness was opened toward the close of the last century when psychoanalysis made its formal debut. This discipline, combining science and intuition, presented the possibility of radically increasing awareness by providing a way of achieving a deepened insight into man's nature. Moreover, by developing tools for the elimination of those functions and processes which previously served to narrow the field of consciousness, it enabled men, as never before, to overcome numerous handicaps to the realization of their age-old ambitions for enlargement.

It is due largely to psychoanalysis that we now know wherein lie the springs of behavior. They are, it seems, in the unconscious, in that vast and heretofore inaccessible area of the psyche fashioned from personal and racial experience. Powered from this remote source, all of our activities broadly reflect the contradictory impulses, the conflicting passions and the warring appetites that strive for expression in word, deed or thought throughout life. We are thus manipulated from within by immense forces of which we are unaware, directed by strivings, urges and unfulfilled needs that move us more surely, and determine our actions more certainly, than the actual demands of reality or the logical necessities of our environment. However, by the extension of consciousness through the new knowledge now available to us, men can free themselves from this slavery and bring both reason and choice, at last, to bear upon their lives.

Awareness, as I have written, is essentially a matter of increasing cortical control over action, of insuring that we are not incapacitated by infantile and primitive compulsions. It can be inculcated in our young by methods of training and education that have been developed correlative with progress in psychoanalysis.

The first requirement for promoting awareness is that parents and teachers who undertake the instruction of children themselves obtain sufficient self-knowledge to avoid making those of whom they have charge the pawns of their own unresolved unconscious strivings. We have recently become acutely concerned with this problem, and have learned to regard it as a formidable hazard of child-training. Too often, it happens that the young, under the guise of education, are merely instructed in ways of carrying out the desires (sometimes forbidden and repressed) of their tutors, and given little opportunity to develop freely according to their own potential or design. Attention to this very real danger, attention proceeding from the care that will follow self-knowledge on the part of teachers and parents, will serve to decrease it significantly.

There is a second prerequisite for those who would assist the young toward awareness. It is imperative that they recognize the peril, and resist the temptation, to capture the minds of their charges by utilizing the functions and organs of natural processes —sexual, digestive, and eliminative—for the establishment of unconscious controls over young lives entrusted to them. Intimately related to the eventual formation of character and the psychological health of a developing organism, such processes require profound understanding and methods of management liberated from deep-rooted prejudices or passions. They form a ready-made beach-head from which an assault can be launched against the freedom of a maturing personality, and as such deserve especially delicate handling.

Once these instructional conditions are satisfied,

training toward awareness is possible with children. In the main, it should consist of the exploitation of every available opportunity to inform the child of the sources of his behavior and to habituate him in the exercise of continuous self-examination. In this manner, as he grows, the greater part of his action will come under conscious supervision, and he will gradually establish control over his own destiny.

Of all the requirements for the rearing and educating of a mature person, awareness is the most difficult to provide for, since it depends so much on the prior mental health and maturity of parents and teachers. The burden rests most heavily upon them; their self-knowledge and their willingness to forego dominance over the malleable minds in their care are the crucial factors involved. But awareness is a central attribute of persons who can exploit the rebellious instinct positively. By eliminating the directive influence of the unconscious and extending the range of consciousness, reason is brought to bear upon living. If a generation of men possessed this capacity alone, they could make an amazing world.

Identity is the second attribute of the positive rebel. It follows awareness and consists of a solidly grounded sense of self, a personal and highly integrated concept of individuality. Technically, identity is considered to be a function of the ego and is composed of all of those traits and reactions by which self-hood is established and recognized. Since an ego is presumed to be a part of the personality of each of us, it may appear odd to name identity as a highly desirable quality and one that is quite rare in contemporary society. Nevertheless, this seems to be the case.

Let us begin by noting that identity is absent from disturbed persons. In the struggle between the basic, instinctive layer of the personality and the repressive forces of society represented by what psychologists call the super-ego, the self or ego is caught as between two grinding millstones. It eventually gives way, and there emerges the sad but notorious spectacle of the person who either believes himself to be other than he is or a lost and unidentified fragment of ego-less matter.

The ego-less state, however, is not confined to the disordered of mind, but is to be discovered also among certain psychopathic types and profusely among Mass Men. With the former, because of faulty rearing the boundaries of the self have been rendered co-extensive with the world, so that it becomes impossible for that self to split off from the environment. The self, therefore, is never realized—a factor which, by the way, seems to account for the inability of such people to distinguish between "mine and thine" and so leads them into the commission of illegalities. As for Mass Men, in them the ego has become so stupefied by conditioning toward submission to persons or ideas of authoritarian character that it comes to occupy only a small portion of the total psychic geography.

In the modern world, under overwhelming pressures toward conformity, regimentation and authoritarianism, there is to be observed a definite trend toward loss of identity. It is a fact that many people do not really know who or what they are. During the course of their lives they fail to acquire a deep conviction of personal distinction, an independent ego. Instead, they habitually attempt to fit themselves into the prevailing pattern, whatever that may be at a given time. Chameleon-like, they alter themselves toward the model image popularized by their conformist institutions. Unidentified in a fundamental sense, they become what any specific situation demands that they become, what it is popular to be, or what it is expedient to be. The moment alone determines the role they are to play, and were it not for their distinguishing names, most men of our time could hardly be told off as persons. Moreover, apart from their names, such identifying data as they possess identifies them with institutions rather than with special qualities or attributes: they are, in short, not persons but Elks, Rotarians, Democrats, Presbyterians, Odd Fellows, Catholics, Optimists, A.F.L.'ers—anything the cards they carry in their wallets tell them to be. The selves of modern men are, indeed, many—and they assume them like masks to meet the passing requirements of a moment.

A fully developed and individualized sense of self, a strong and uncontaminated ego, is a necessity for maturity. There can be no security without it, either for the person or the society he inhabits. To insure that a child is directed toward maturity, that it has a chance to become a person in its own right and not by the paternalistic fiat of some alien organization, requires that it be encouraged toward self-hood from the very earliest days of its infancy and throughout its entire time of growth. This can be done; but, once more, its success depends upon the tutors to whose instruction and example the child is exposed. Parents and teachers have, first, to be willing to *allow* the child to become a person; they have to *permit* him to acquire individual identity. From this base, it then becomes possible to assist the child toward a knowledge of who and what he really is, in himself, apart from *their* conscious or unconscious allegiances, who and what he is apart from *their* dominating wishes and concerns.

Identity is the secure conviction of uniqueness and individuality that is the birth-right of every person, a conviction that, if respected and nourished, will one day enable the child who acquires it to take his place as an instrument in what Julian Huxley has described as the great human orchestra.

The third item in the psychic profile of the positive rebel is *skepticism*. By this is meant the mental habit of doubt, of questioning, and the corresponding refusal to accept anything on the basis of faith or authority.

If one factor can be held accountable for the evident distress of contemporary society, it is the

creeping paralysis that has overtaken us subsequent
to our loss of the capacity for doubt. Faith has played
a large part in our increasing social despair and, unless we take heed, may prove to be the ultimate
weapon in the undoing of the West. I do not write
here merely of religious faith—although the famous
"I believe just because it is absurd" of religionists has
been an outstanding suppressor of reason for centuries—but of all faith founded on the inhibition of
thought and the declaration of "truth" by sole virtue
of authority. I write, that is, of faith in politicians, of
faith in the written word, of faith in uniforms, of faith
in the stereotypes and myths that so largely govern
our lives today.

From the moment of birth the ordinary course
of events provides a person with already-fashioned
sets of opinions, ready-made articles of belief, and
prefabricated systems of conduct to which he is required to subscribe without hesitation or question.
Under pressure first from his parents and later from
various delegates of society, the child is made to fit
himself into the prevailing social pattern and to bring
both thought and behavior into line with the prescribed mode. Criticism of anything basic is largely
denied him, and if he at any time exercises his inborn freedom to question the predigested equations
on which he is forced to order his affairs, he can usually anticipate censorship if not total rejection. Thus
it transpires that the capacity for skepticism is stunted

from birth in most instances, and the taproot of creativity and progress destroyed.

Authority has every reason to fear the skeptic, for authority can rarely survive in the face of doubt. Consequently, it puts a premium on faith and pays it the highest homage possible: faith is the source of its power.

Resistance to tyranny, whether over the body or the mind, originates in the question, in the expression of doubt. Therefore, it is important to preserve the natural function of inquiry, of why-asking. Today this function, this hallmark of maturity, is being suborned by conformist institutions to whose advantage it is or will be that men everywhere renounce criticism. So successful have they become in our time that the questioner is now not only regarded by others with horror, but he himself experiences anxiety at his own presumption. We cannot preserve the freedoms that are threatened—or recover those we have lost—in such a climate.

The child can be—must be—reared in the exercise of skepticism. From birth he is provided with a natural proclivity for what we analysts call reality-testing. This native curiosity can be employed in his training as the apparatus for the encouragement of inquisitiveness, for discovery, for the untrammeled, independent exploration of his universe. Central to his instruction in living must be made the dictum: "Take nothing for granted—find out!" But to

implement this educational principle requires an unusual degree of discipline by parents and teachers
over themselves. It demands a willingness to grant
children a degree of liberty hardly tolerable to most
of us. Moreover, to encourage skepticism necessitates
exposing our own cherished notions to the possibility
of rejection. We have not only to re-examine our attitudes and opinions, but also to prevent ourselves from
communicating to our young the irrationalities we
have inherited or acquired, irrationalities which may
have become, in some cases, the foundations of our
very lives. But this price is not too high; for if the
child can obtain from our efforts the mental habit of
skepticism, we will have given him the means to
preserve his freedom.

Responsibility is the fourth distinguishing trait
of the mature person. It is a matter that presents two
aspects or levels, one personal, the other social.

With mankind, nature has attempted something
new. By providing the human animal with an apparatus at the apex of his nervous system for centraliz-
ing, organizing and co-ordinating information, she
has prepared him for more than recording facts or
reacting to them. Among other functions mediated by
the brain of man are the capacity for understanding
the relationships of separate items of information
and, above all, predicting consequences. Man, therefore, is endowed with a prophetic sense, an ability to
foretell, within limits, the possible outcome of many
of his activities. This renders him the sole consciously

responsible animal among the forms of life. As a prophet, he naturally acquires accountability for large areas of his behavior, since he is informed in advance as to the results and thus offered the possibility of choice. From an evolutionary point of view, the implications of this radical innovation are tremendous. It means that the animal so endowed is equipped to take charge of its own destiny and is no longer, like forms without prophetic ability, at the mercy of apparently blind, designless natural forces.

Responsibility is, therefore, biologically founded, and it is to the fact of his answerability that the child must be reared. The prophetic sense demands exercise and development. With practice, it can extend itself over a far wider range of human behavior than it is now permitted to occupy, and opens the possibility for bringing increasingly large areas of the future under control. Preliminary steps toward the development of responsibility on the personal level in the child require that, in his early training, emphasis be placed upon those experiences which are the ordinary consequences of his behavior. As we allow our young to experiment with life and obtain knowledge of the results of their actions, their sense of responsibility increases. Within the limits of his safety, such training has to be instituted and maintained throughout the years of growth. From it, he will acquire numerous benefits, one of which will be the development of a natural control over unconscious motivants and the spontaneous inhibition of those predominantly selfish desires that ordinarily (or otherwise) operate mechanically and in disregard of consequences to the self and others.

On the social level the facts regarding responsibility are similarly clear. Each human is appointed his brother's keeper at birth by virtue of his possession of a humanoid type of brain. Because every act involves other persons, and most if not all actions at the time of their inception include some foreknowledge of their potential effects, a network of responsibility exists among all members of the species. These tenuous strands of inter-human accountability are strengthened, furthermore, by inborn capacities (also lacking to a large degree among other animal forms) for sympathy and empathy based upon resemblances in the structure and function of all people. Three elements, then—responsibility, sympathy, and empathy —support the instinctual, survival-dictated need to come together and assist the formation of societies. The mutual dependency that arises from the gathering of individuals into groups, and the interlocking effect of all the units, further establishes the responsibility of every person for every other person.

To this solidarity, to this interwoven complex of responsibility arising solely from the fact that he is human, the child has to be reared. Because the natural architecture of his body and the inborn biomechanics of his being incline him anyhow in the direction indicated, little difficulty will be encountered by tutors who attempt to assist nature to realize itself by increasing the child's social awareness and sense of responsibility. There is no alternative: each man *is* every man's brother and keeper, part of an organic whole in which he is an individual as well as an important piece.

Employment is a fifth characteristic of maturity. It is a word I have chosen to indicate an attitude toward life, an attitude of affirmative dedication to existence, of profound and complete participation in living.

I do not wish to imply by the use of the term "employed" anything that has to do with productivity or the use of energy for economic and other satisfactions. In my view the world is not, as some seem to think, a basket-weaving class, and I have little respect for philosophies which suggest that we are here to keep busy. By employed I mean, rather, the active assumption of life as a vocation consisting of the utter devotion of one's self to evolution, the total participation of the personality in the on-going parade. The employed man, therefore, is the man pledged to progress, defined as those advances against all limitations or barriers to a break-through into the next dimension of evolution, whatever that dimension may be. The employed man, moreover, is the man who, to expedite this aim, utilizes all of his innate and acquired capabilities and potentialities, and by their use develops, enlarges and capitalizes on them.

Such a man as I have described adheres to a viewpoint concerning himself and existence that contrasts sharply with the outlook that prevails in contemporary society. He conceives of his life as an experiment in the laboratory of the cosmos, an experiment conducted toward the eventual achievement of some hardly conceivable form of life of which he is, perhaps, a forerunner. Himself he regards as no more —and no less—than one of an infinite number of efforts to become that form of the future. So he treasures the small differences between himself and others, reflecting (if he wishes) that these are being tested in life's crucible to determine their suitability for the magnificent cosmic task. Being and action are also precious to him and significant in the highest degree *just because* his personal existence is a kind of "experimental run" of the qualities that comprise his person. In this the employed man finds his own meaning and the meaning of his fellows.

From the fact of his employment in the sense I have explained, the individual who possesses this spirited quality derives an ethic superior in every way to whatever ethic reigns in the society he finds himself. Its baseline is life, which it affirms through love and respect. Also, it is an immutable ethic; since its propositions are derived from the absolute nature of man and his relations with his fellows and the world, it does not change with every vagrant social, religious, moral, economic or political breeze.

Finally, to be employed provides the fortunate possessor of this major attribute of maturity with a dynamic to resist the destructive instincts. In the great dichotomy of the basic drives, employment joins the life-preservative forces. Affirmative of life and dedicated to draining the last drops of vitality in order to conclude the individual experiment, it struggles endlessly against the tides of dissolution and decay. To it, I believe, goes the final victory.

It is possible, I think, to engender an attitude of employment within the maturing organism. By example and instruction a child can be encouraged toward a philosophy of this kind, a philosophy that will give him a sense of the great and abiding mission of his life. Such an attitude, to my mind, replaces formal religion with something that is not only healthier psychologically, but of far more spiritual value. It dispenses with the collective illusion our religions of dogma, form and ritual are now and always will be. It does away with the current necessity for a supernatural, for the wishful and dubious comforts of a belief in personal immortality. In addition, the attitude of employment counteracts fear, replaces the unknown by the known, regulates life, and controls conduct not through the evasion of responsibility by projection on forces outside and hidden from the self, but from within. Above all, it preserves the dignity of man, for it requires no subservience, no debasing rituals of submission, no appeasements, no sacrifices, no need for atonement. By blending nature, mind, and instinct, employment produces the perfect "religion" for man—the "religion" of Life.

The final quality I am able to name in this slim

catalogue of traits of the mature person is *tension*. This is a much-abused word that, in the modern lexicon, has become entangled semantically with wholly negative connotations. Currently, it is descriptive of a state of tautness (regarded as "bad") as opposed to a state of relaxation (regarded as "good"). As an attribute of maturity, however, it is used to denote a condition of dissatisfaction with things as they are, an alertness to reality which takes cognizance of the gap between what is and what can and should be, and an internal restlessness or discontent conjoined with a determination to promote change.

Men of today fear to be tense. They have been subverted by the folly of passivity, seduced into the specious luxury of unconcern. So-called authorities sagely advise them that "tension is bad for us," that "we must relax," and "stop taking things so seriously." Solicitude, indignation, involvement—these have become crimes; the "take it easy," "to hell with it," and "I should care" attitudes receive praise and the recommendation of experts. Tension-reducers, soporifics, sedatives and hypnotics flood an eager market to the amount of fifteen million units each day in the United States alone. Libraries of "entertainment," "relaxation," and "mind-easement" are ground out by the public presses and the mass media of motion pictures, radio and television every hour . . . The appalling tragedy of this must impress all who have read this far: the untense mind, the unconcerned mind, the dulled, relaxed, uncaring mind is a travesty of human nature.

To rear the child to be tense in the special sense of the definition I have proposed infuses him with a knowledge of existing reality and a corresponding desire to alter it constructively. It entails dispelling at their source the insane propositions nourished by so many of our social institutions that change is wrong, that we are obliged to adjust and conform, that this world as it stands must be preserved. By choking off such delusions through correct instruction before they crystallize in all their pernicious error, we can not only promote the development of individuals dedicated to progressive change, but we can provide endless causes for the utilization of the rebellious instinct. There is no reason to fear tension. To make the child tense is to feed a nature that can realize itself only through the positive exercise of its potential for betterment and improvement. It is to call upon his resources, activate his capabilities, and command his potentialities. From mind-in-tension he will be rewarded with a better, a more exciting, and a richer life.

The foregoing appear to me to be the chief qualities that define the mature person. These are the traits that must be incorporated somehow into the personality of the child for him to make personal and social capital of his instinct of rebellion. Admittedly, they are characteristics rare among us today; and, sadly, with the passing of each day they seem to become more rare. About how to turn this tide I, for one, have only the vaguest ideas. The pedagogy of freedom is a novel adventure for the mind, and the few principles I have outlined here represent but the first and highly tentative gropings toward it. But I believe profoundly that the tide can be turned, that we can learn how to be rebellious and how to rear and educate our youth to maturity. The key, I suggest, lies with ourselves; it lies in an initial act of liberation from the myth of adjustment. With this act, we manifest our own maturity and obtain the *right* to instruct others.